WEEPING WALLS

Inspired by True Events

Bobby Karim

authorHOUSE®

AuthorHouse™
1663 Liberty Drive
Bloomington, IN 47403
www.authorhouse.com
Phone: 1 (800) 839-8640

This is a work of fiction. All of the characters, names, incidents, organizations, and dialogue in this novel are either the products of the author's imagination or are used fictitiously.

Published by AuthorHouse 04/19/2019

ISBN: 978-1-7283-0907-1 (sc)
ISBN: 978-1-7283-0909-5 (hc)
ISBN: 978-1-7283-0908-8 (e)

Library of Congress Control Number: 2019904837

Print information available on the last page.

Dedication

They say that life is precious, but it is only precious when there are people to share it with. Anyone can live, but few can live a life free of companionship. Whether be it a wife, sister, brother, mother, or father, we all desperately need someone to call our own. As people, we strive to have a genuine companion as it is difficult to hold the line of solitude. This book is dedicated to the people who have impacted my positive energy in the precious gift of life. Through struggles, hardships, misery, and pain, they have been there to support and celebrate the gift of my life. My wife, mother, sisters, brothers, son, and daughters have been the driving force behind the encouragement and strength to find my way. They have sincerely shown me that the bond of a family is the strongest of all and that it can withstand the harshest of impediments that can obstruct the path to a precious life. Together, we effortlessly encourage the faith, valor, and strength, that provide the stability and sanctuary of our familial bond. Cherished are those who sincerely believe in the potency and unanimity of a family.

Prologue

On a dark, dismal evening, about 7:30 p.m., as I sat alone in a small park on the edge of town, the wind started to increase its intensity. I could see very low clouds beginning to drift across the sky. The leaves on the ground had begun to kite around, making rustling sounds. I could feel a chill from the air entering through the buttoned spaces on my hooded cotton shirt. I hadn't gone out expecting such a beautiful day to become so increasingly dreary as it wore on.

A few hours had passed and I was still there in solitude, only now, the winds had calmed and the night had turned into peaceful bliss. The moon finally showed itself and lit up the sky. There was silence all around, not a whisper in the wind nor a murmur of the nightly insects that ruled. I could hear myself breathe, that's when I realized something had terribly gone wrong. The forces that lay beyond anyone's trivial imagination, beyond the explanations of societal norms were at work. The wings of unimaginable evil, it seemed, had started to flutter its cruel wings somewhere once again. Someone somewhere was going to be seduced into immense agony and hatred. Their life was going to be forever altered and never would someone close, ever come to terms with the comprehension of such dark and evil forces.

Our understanding of such forces will always be met with skepticism, not because we are mere humans but we lack the ability, or more appropriately, we suppress the ability to entertain the education of a power greater than ourselves.

We make attempts to test tube every occurrence, every oddity, hoping that there'd be logic and explanatory data. We are afraid to face an undeniable reality, a reality that exists amongst us but was created by the ultimate of evil power that was summoned by our own brethren.

As my mind drifted and the wisdom that I had gained started addressing different questions, I wondered to myself if there would be anyone to help the next unexpected victim of such atrocities that I have endured. I had come to understand and realize over the past few months, that it's not or wasn't a one-time occurrence but it's simultaneously occurring in hundreds, if not thousands, of places throughout our comfortable world. An evil within our society, amongst our leaders and our innocent children. I wondered then, what I could do to help such victims. With a sword, with a gun – I couldn't; but the experience and the wisdom I had gained most certainly would be of help to the less fortunate. After all, I am breathing today. I may not ever be one hundred percent anymore but I am blessed enough to let it be known to as many as I could; to educate my friends, my family, and the people of the world, about an uncertain and despicable evil that challenges the beliefs and foundation of what life is constructed upon. My eyes then closed, and like pressing the rewind button on a video recorder, I returned to the beginning, to the beginning, to the beginning...

Chapter One

The Christmas season had come along in full swing. Kevin, Linda, Anna and I were looking forward to spending our first Christmas at our new home, our first house. It was a beautiful two-family brick house that sat on a peaceful and quiet street in a family friendly neighborhood. An elegant white fence separated the concrete sidewalk that created a path to our layered front step. A bay window at the front allowed ample sunlight in. During the evenings, we sipped on homemade hot chocolate within the confines of a very large inner seating area.

There were many reasons why we considered this Christmas season one of the best yet. Linda was going to celebrate her first birthday in the first week of the New Year and Anna and I had sacrificed a lot the past few months to make owning our new home a reality. I had worked two jobs and Anna completed many hours of overtime to save a little extra. Everything that had led up to this time of year had gone very well for us. It was indeed a time for celebrating.

Linda was eleven months old; she was the most beautiful, adorable baby girl I had ever seen. Her ebony black hair, her large brown eyes, and her naturally tan complexion made her beauty so much more complimenting. She was full of energy, full of life, and full of a dreamful future of inspiration that enabled the strength within me. After she was born, there was a feeling of completion within me. I had felt that our little family was completing itself; she had brought closure to all the wants and needs that I could only have dreamed of.

Kevin was two years old and had always been the pride and joy of the family with his jet-black hair, round face, and chubby cheeks. Most noticeably was his general built, he was only two but looked like four. He was chubby for his age which made him a target by the entire family for mischief. He was very fun loving, wickedly playful, and enjoyed every moment of his so very short existence thus far. Kevin and I were ultimately close, we were attached to the hip. Everywhere I went he was right there with his sister by his side. They were very close and even though Linda was filled with innocence and the advantage of youthful ignorance, she was evidently but subconsciously jealous of him. She followed him everywhere because she knew he was her protector, her big brother.

Anna, my wife, was very attractive, weighed about one hundred and thirty pounds, and was lightly complexioned. She possessed a great sense of humor, something that made me fall in love with her instantaneously. She was very family oriented, loved entertaining visitors, and going out and having quality family time together. Anna was an excellent cook, there wasn't anything you could have thought of, or felt like eating, that she did not have a recipe for. She was born in Guyana and migrated to New York at the tender age of fourteen. She attended school and also worked to assist her family with their various needs after arriving in New York.

As for me, I was twenty-eight years old, full of life, energy, and enthusiasm. I was born in the beautiful island of Trinidad, the twin island of Tobago, and migrated to New York in the winter of nineteen-ninety. I worked in the furniture industry then, before I went into transportation. Anna and I recently got married and we had now started a wonderful family. We had plans, goals, and objectives that we were working towards. Every day brought about a new sense of achievement and perspective. I enjoyed the familial moments we spent together. I enjoyed cooking, entertaining guests, and being out at the various destinations we visited as a family. We were simple people making an attempt to live free, live happily, and provide for our children. Nothing was of more importance to both Anna and I. We knew we were on our way to achieving the typical "American Dream." There was no self-doubt that existed since we had planned our lives carefully from the moment we exchanged our vows and had visions of our future. Anna and I had seemed destined to meet each other and be together. I fell in love with her the second I had first seen her. The complete aura of her presence sent sparks throughout my entire system and I immediately fell in love with her.

Although Anna and I were of different countries, we were of the same Indian background. Guyana and Trinidad are both very diversified in their cultures and religions. The population in both countries consists largely of Christians, Hindus, and Muslims. We were all familiar with each other's religion due to the diversity that laid within the small but knitted communities. Due to this heterogeneity, cultures and religions were equally educated and practiced amongst the people. Within the immediate families, we consisted largely of Muslims and Hindus but we were all very educated with that of the Christian religion as well. This multiplicity allowed for many inter-religion relationships and cultural exchanges of likes and dislikes within society. There were exchanges of foods, ethnic beliefs, and understandings that meshed the bonds created from a domestic togetherness.

Anna and I came to a decision that we weren't going to keep any family gathering on Christmas day; however, we were going to celebrate Linda's first birthday with much grandeur, being that it was just a couple of weeks after Christmas. We were planning every day in the last two weeks of December and the beginning of the New Year. We needed to get special foods for the various people we invited. One of my sisters followed the Hindu religion due to marrying into a Hindu family and the other a Muslim due to marrying into a Muslim family. They all had certain foods that were taboo so Anna and I promised that we would make everything perfect. We shopped for decorations of mutual likes for everyone and the specificity of each individual that was invited. It was important that all who were invited would be comfortable and had a theme of their own beliefs represented at the party. Everyone was given invitations; my mother, brother, both my sisters, and their husbands. Anna's mom, dad, and her two brothers were living in the basement apartment of our house, yet out of formality, they were officially given invitations as well. Anna and I also invited a few friends from our respective jobs to participate in a gathering for the ages.

The day had finally arrived, the 6th of January, 2001. It was Linda's birthday. I had taken the day off from work and gotten up very early that morning along with Anna. There were lots of preparations to be made. It was such an exciting day. The cleaning, the decorations, the cooking; everything was being tended to without any disruptions. On this gorgeous day, everything automatically fell right into place. All chores were so harmlessly and efficiently being taken care of. I remember thinking, "This day is definitely meant to be."

Later that afternoon, the preparations were completed. The living room was entirely decorated with balloons, streamers, and various colorful garlands. The stacked table was laid with food and an assortment of alcoholic and non-alcoholic beverages. The multi-colored stenciled art that made the cream walls their background brought about a jubilant and festive mood. Anna, Linda, Kevin, and I, David, were already bathed and dressed and laid in wait for our expected guests. They were sporadic in showing up but it was about seven o' clock that evening when everyone finally did. We were all having a great time; there were lots of food and drinks, a great musical ensemble, dancing, and, most importantly, the enjoyment of a family gathering celebrating the birthday of our much-beloved daughter.

Everyone seemed to be having a great time and enjoying themselves. I'd take little glances across the packed room, homing in on each individual at two or three-second intervals. My eyes laid to rest on Anna's mother, Lucy. She stood next to the glass china in the dining room in a floral-patterned dress that provided a beauty far beyond the backdrop of her very dark and wrinkled skin. Her hair glittered from the abundance of white and her breasts hung below her abdominal line, exaggerated by the seams of the dress she wore. Her sunken eyes provided no assistance to her cold, sinister, and unforgiving ogle as her head turned towards Anna with a befuddled look. She didn't appear to be very happy. She'd stare at all in attendance with a sign of disgust and envy written on her face. I didn't make anything of it at the time because she was in her sixties, very old fashioned, and wasn't very fond of parties and such.

Anna was her daughter and she cared deeply for her. They did everything together. I got concerned at times due to how close they were. I worried that if anything were to ever happen to Lucy, Anna would become very emotionally depressed. Anna had a profound love for her and they seemed inseparable. My mother and sister had always warned, and made fun, that I should never let an in-law move into the same house where I lived but I didn't want to disrupt the relationship Anna shared with her mother. They were never too fond of Lucy and only pretended to have respected and cared for her for mine and Anna's sake. They thought she was pretentious so they never forged a more meaningful relationship with her. They had always believed that she was not Anna's biological mother. Lucy's and Anna's traits did not match. There were many distinguishing contrasts to their personalities, their physical features, and their general demeanor.

About half-past eight I saw her walk over to Anna and slyly say something to her. I was across the room and did not hear what was being communicated, especially with the music being so loud. She appeared to be very short on words but straight to the point. Anna did not seem happy but nodded her head in approval. Lucy then proceeded toward the kitchen at the rear of the house where there was an entrance to the basement apartment where they lived. She slammed the door shut and was on her way. The guests did not appear distracted due to the music but I saw her clearly from where I stood.

The basement apartment in which they stayed was converted from empty space into an operational two-bedroom, full kitchen and bath apartment. Anna and I had several opinionated conversations about what should have been done about the extra space the basement provided. I had wanted to use it for storage but Anna thought that it would help if we converted the space into an apartment. She thought we could have rented it out to generate a little extra income to assist with the mortgage payments. I finally agreed with her and we completed the renovations in short order. Around that time, Lucy, Richard, and Daniel were in the process of looking for an apartment and it was hesitantly decided by Anna and I that we would rent it to them. Lucy had pitched to us that she would assist with the kids, being that she would be so close by. That idea had appealed to Anna and I so we decided to rent the apartment at a discounted rate to them, rather than to strangers.

The night of the party moved along enjoyably slow and around midnight or so, our very welcomed guests began to depart to their homes. It was about two a.m. when the remaining guests had decided to leave.

Kevin and Linda were allowed to stay up a little later than usual so I took them up the stairs, gave them a quick bath, and took them to their respective rooms. I then returned downstairs to help Anna get the place cleaned up. I knew that she would not have waited until morning. She was conscientious of keeping the place tidy and would have wanted it done right away so she'd have a peaceful night's rest. While in the kitchen tending to the dishes, I asked her what her mother had said to her and why she had left the party so early. Anna responded by saying that her mother wasn't feeling that great and wanted to rest a little early. I didn't make anything of it because she was elderly and I totally understood. We then finished up the cleaning and turned in for the night. As I laid in bed, I thanked God for making everything work out so well and thanked Him all so much for having blessed me with all the happiness He had showered upon my family and I.

Little did I know, that night would be the last night we were going to have so much fun in months and months to follow. Little did I know, that for months to come, they would be filled with pain, grief, and so much sorrow. How was I to know that such a monster of a storm was about to take hold of my family? To this day, I am yet to recover from what took place in the months following Linda's first birthday. The light which had shone upon my family was about to lose its glow and allow the darkness to slowly crawl in.

Chapter Two

Anna and her family were from the country of Guyana. They were traditional and believed in the old ways. Family traditions and customs were held in high regard there. They believed in adopting their culture into the modern world hoping that it would bring about a togetherness which was sometimes lacking in our foreign society.

In the few days that followed the party, Anna's mom, Lucy, decided to make a sudden trip to Guyana. She asked Anna to accompany her and she also wanted to take the kids along. In the second week of January, Anna came to me to seek my approval to go along on the trip.

Anna and I were very close. All the years we spent together, we had learned how to get along, not only as husband and wife, but also as best friends. Because of this reason, there were many people that respected us. The love and friendship that we shared were admired by all. It's very hard to believe, but we never fought; problems always seemed to have worked themselves out. Friends and family would tell us they've never seen a relationship that was more meant to be than ours. I always told my friends that I could have left Anna by herself on an island of men and I knew nothing would happen. There was a special trust I had developed for her due to her background and her successful and worthy nature. It was a relationship borne in heaven and one that was etched in the ideology of man and wife. Due to her family's traditions, they were having her marriage arranged to someone else, someone the family had also known and was close to. Anna chose love marriage over an arranged one; she chose me. She went against family traditions and opted for love, our love. Everyone knew that the existence of our relationship was not one of normality but one of rarity and longevity and it was forged from the God of love. Anna had always promised that she would never marry someone who smoked, who drank, and she never would have gone against her parent's wishes. She went against all her family and against her own beliefs because she fell in love. I, fortunately, was the one she fell in love with. I smoked, occasionally drank, and did not adhere to any one particular religion, yet she fell in love with me. We had met at a furniture store where I worked and through circumstances of chance, I was the one who delivered the furniture she had purchased. That's where our budding relationship had begun its nurture and bloom. I spent hours at her house assembling the various pieces of an entertainment center. Although her family being present, I was able to get in a couple of words here and there. By the time we had finished assembling everything, I had built up the courage to ask her out, but she referred me to her father, Richard. She said in their family, I had to ask her parents. Richard, although being in his sixties, was very built and appeared tough. There was a certain swagger to him that created a fear from his demeanor and his huge upper body. He had worked very hard in Guyana and had gained respect from his peers and family. Anna wouldn't have gone out with me if the permission wasn't sought for and granted. I built up the courage and finally asked her father and he said that it was fine. From that day onward, we never looked back; I had become well-liked by Richard, Lucy, and Anna's entire family. There were many times spent with her family at the park, at the beach, and at various family gatherings. After all, we had gotten engaged in the backyard of their family's home with much pomp and great attendance from both families and friends.

I didn't anticipate any issues with her and the kids accompanying her mother, so it was agreed that they'd go. Anna and her mother made all the necessary arrangements for their trip and they were scheduled to depart out of John F. Kennedy International Airport in approximately two weeks, on January 20th. I was an illegal immigrant that migrated from Trinidad and Tobago and lived in New York since the time I arrived in 1990. After marrying, Anna had submitted the necessary paperwork so I can become naturalized. My green card and essential travel documents weren't finalized yet, so I was unable to accompany them even though I wanted to. At the time, we were a little strapped for cash and I would have probably stayed back anyway, to avoid the costly trip. In the following two weeks, Anna spent a lot of time with her mother, they were out a lot and even when home, she'd be in the basement apartment. I knew that preparations needed to be made; shopping, planning, and all the arrangements for their visit to Guyana.

The day had finally come for them to leave. Anna, Lucy, and the kids were very busy making last minute preparations, checking to make sure they weren't leaving anything behind. Finally, they got everything together and we were off to JFK. After arriving at the airport and checking-in, we all sat in the waiting area prior to the security checkpoint. Kevin and Linda were very excited to be going on an airplane. Every opportunity that presented itself, I was able to give both of them many hugs and kisses. Since they were brought into this world, they were never away from me for more than a day. I held Linda in my arms and Kevin sat on my shaking knee. Anna, her mother, and myself were indulged in conversations of things to do when they were gone, when over the intercom came the dreaded call of departure for their flight. We all stood up and said our goodbyes, exchanged hugs and kisses, and they were off. Not even twenty feet had separated me from them when Anna turned around and yelled, "David! David!" and she came running towards me with tears in her eyes, grabbed onto me, and squeezed me very tightly. It's not because she had never held onto me this tightly before but, there was a deeper meaning behind this particular embrace. We were going to be apart; the family was going to be temporarily separated. I returned her meaningful embrace while attempting to remain strong. She told me the trip will be very difficult for her because we were never apart and she doesn't know how she'll cope with being away from me for three weeks. Tears had also filled my eyes, but being a man, they never actually left them. The muscles that controlled the glands of my eyes were being flexed and they kept the tears from flowing. I was never fond of goodbyes so I tried doing everything as quickly as possible so the moment wouldn't be prolonged or as tense for either of us. The human element in me was attempting to suppress the emotional torture in order to save me from the struggles of coping with the trauma of what my heart was feeling. The kids and I waved each other goodbye and I gave Anna a very tight hug and a big kiss before I speedily left toward the parking garage.

On my way home, all the tears that I had held from flowing began pouring out and wouldn't stop. It had not even been a half an hour, and here I was, pulled off to the side of the road weeping my eyes out. I felt broken; there were strings attached to my being that were unraveling across the sea. The further I moved away from them, the emptier I felt. I missed them so much. I sat in the car for about an hour before I got halfway composed and then mustered the strength to continue my short but lengthy journey home.

The night they left, I walked around the house. It was so desolate and quiet; no little noises, no little mischiefs brewing, not a wife saying "Honey come to bed," not anything. It was very strange, I had never felt so alone and separated from everything in my entire life. It took me forever to sleep but after a lot of tossing and turning, I finally did.

The next morning, I got up, got dressed, and was on my way to the post office when I saw Richard, Anna's father, and Daniel, Anna's brother. They asked if Anna had called to inform me of their arrival in Guyana. I shook my head implying no and they told me not to worry, they were sure that she'd call. I wasn't quite worried so off I went to the post office and they to wherever they were off to. There were a few errands to run and I made quick work of them to ensure a faster return to the house.

I got home a little after three that afternoon and waited patiently by the phone. Just about five o'clock, the phone rang. It was Anna, she had called to let me know that they had arrived safely and all was well. It was a regular conversation as could be. We exchanged pleasantries, Linda and Kevin were both given an opportunity to say hi to me, and we spoke about the flight and their journey to where they were staying. After a few minutes, we all exchanged goodbyes and hung up. I continued perusing through the channels on the television in hope of becoming drowsy. I did not intend to go through another difficult night struggling to fall asleep.

That night when I went to bed, the strangest and most unexpected things happened. I was lying in bed and suddenly felt scared. What was I scared of? I myself did not know. A feeling of fright had empowered me and suddenly I was vulnerable to weakness, weaknesses that I'm normally protected from and indestructible against. I have always taken pride in myself for having a strong mind that couldn't be broken. In my younger years, growing up in a third-world country provided many struggles and there was a need to make yourself strong to cope with the harsh nature of society.

I felt as though there were hundreds of eyes leering at me. It was unbelievably eerie. My heart started pounding, I asked myself silently, "What the hell is going on?" I was never this afraid before. I felt as though something wasn't right; everything appeared to be disoriented, out of place, in shambles, and confusing. Whenever my eyes blinked shut, I would sense the leering eyes and I felt accompanied and violated in my private bedroom. I forced my eyes tightly closed and recited my nightly prayer. Just as a young child would do, I retreated under the thick blanket, held the pillow tightly over my head, and forced upon myself thoughts of pleasantness. That night, again, I did not realize when I had fallen asleep but, after a lot of uneasiness, I somehow did.

The next morning, I got up, showered, got dressed, and went to work. Everything felt awkward, it seemed like the wind had changed direction and nothing seemed normal. There was just not an explanation to what I had felt. I couldn't get a grasp or handle on what was going on. I felt lost, totally confused, and as if I was in another world. I'd be walking and my posture would feel slanted to a degree that was not the same as an average human being. There were signs of disruption but I took no heed to them. I would breathe myself into explanations and give excuses and reasons to disbelieve the faint but obvious signals. Somehow, I managed to get through a very difficult day at work.

After getting home that afternoon, I kept pacing the house, anxiously awaiting Anna's call. It had been a while since I last spoke to my family and it was tormenting me. About seven o' clock that evening, Anna finally called. When she got on the phone, she was crying hysterically. Repeatedly, she was telling me how much she missed me. Constantly crying, she would say, "David, I want to come home, I want to come home." It had only been two days so I tried calming her down but it was of no avail. I kept reassuring her of my love and commitment to her and the kids and that I missed them just as much. Continuously, I verbally comforted her and little by little, the crying subsided and we were finally able to have a mutually comprehensible conversation. I was able to convince her to stay, even though in my heart I wanted nothing more than for them to return. I got a chance to speak with Kevin and Linda. They both missed me so much and I, them. Linda could speak very few words but the way in which they were uttered, I knew. Kevin was older and much more vocal so I spent more time speaking with him. We constantly said, "I love you" and "I love you too" to each other until we hung up the phone.

I had spoken to them and I received an assurance from the person whom I loved so dearly. Although we were countries apart, the bond that existed between us had not died but was healthier and stronger than ever before. However, within me, I knew something was wrong but failed to admit to it myself, failed to accept the reality of what my sixth sense was telling me. Anna had not been like that before. I heard in her voice a feeling of terror, of being emotionally tormented. I convinced myself she was just going through longing from being away from me and everything else that comforted her here in the

United States. From talking to them, I had gotten a small sense of relief, though it didn't last very long.

That night, I felt out of sync. I wasn't in the mood for anything. I did not want to look at television, listen to music, read a book, or do anything for that matter. I tried various things to keep my mind occupied but nothing enticed me nor tickled my fancy. There was nothing that piqued my interest for me to attempt. I felt so empty; it was like drifting into thin air with absolutely no purpose, no objective, and no control. It was a peculiar feeling that I had never gotten before. I did not pay any particular attention to the feelings I was experiencing as I thought they were associated with the fact that I was missing my family and going through the normal emotions of a human being when they are apart from the ones they love. I denied myself the ability to see beyond, to look further than the walls in front of me. Maybe I was scared to find out the truth or maybe I was just a coward.

In Guyana, Anna's family did not possess a phone that she could have used at her convenience. If she wanted to use a telephone, she would need to go to someone, maybe a close neighbor, miles away, or to someone who owns a phone in their locality. She would then have to pay for such services and also use it at that person's convenience. It wasn't my expectation to hear from Anna every day, but I had optimistically hoped that she'd call every other day.

Six very unsettling days had passed and I hadn't heard from Anna. I'd position myself by the telephone every afternoon with the hope that she would call. I was beginning to get angrily worried. As each night passed, I would find it more and more difficult to fall asleep.

About a week later, I laid in bed one night, again struggling to fall asleep. That feeling I had nearly a week ago, was back. I felt scared, even more so than the last time. This time, there wouldn't only be eyes I felt sneering at me, but I had begun hearing voices. They were plentiful and grew louder as each second passed. I did not understand what the whispering voices were communicating but they were irritable and harmoniously disturbing. As the whispers continued, I became increasingly frightened. They brought with them a pestering and ominous presence that had filled a coldness within me. The unwelcomed voices had penetrated my shield and made me susceptible to their intended fear. I squeezed the pillow tightly against my head and drew the blanket closer with the hope of ridding myself of the fear that had begun to settle in. My attempts were futile and the voices continued. I began reciting my prayer over and over and the voices slowly vanished and took the fear with them. With all the time I had for myself, I'd try to decipher what was going on, but no matter what I tried, I was getting more petulant. My brain, it seemed, had become paralyzed from seeing anything more than two inches in front of me. I didn't follow any particular religion but I believed that there was a God and prayed often – before every meal, before going to bed, and whenever I had accomplished something or even having escaped the smallest of perils. I would make sure to acknowledge that it was because of a much greater power rather than believing in coincidence. I possessed a great faith, a strong faith in God, and I've always known that I've gotten this far in life for that reason.

Chapter Three

On the eighth night, I was preparing a sandwich when the phone rang. It was Anna. I was surprised and so happy for I hadn't heard from her in over a week, which had felt like a lifetime to me.

I couldn't stop talking, there were so many questions: "How are you?" "Why didn't you call in such a long time?" "How's Kevin?" "How's Linda?" "Do they miss me?" I never gave Anna a chance to answer. Suddenly, there was a silence, a pause, and then I asked her if she missed me. There was no answer. Anna just held the phone to her ear and humbly cried in a low tone, but never gave an answer. I knew she was there; she wasn't the same, something had changed for the worse. I myself became silent. I stood in the kitchen, still holding the phone while staring at it every so often. I braced myself against the refrigerator and propped myself up against one of the lower cabinet's door, thinking to myself that I had refused to follow my instincts and accept that something was wrong. Anna wasn't herself. She wanted to say something, she wanted to speak but she couldn't. The phone then, without warning, hung up. I kept standing there looking at the phone expecting that an answer would be provided through the dial. I didn't, I couldn't, understand what had just happened. I had never been so hurt like that before. I gently put the phone down and stumbled my way into the family room trying to give myself an explanation for what had just transpired. Time, for me, had stopped. A minute took an hour, a million and more things were going through my head. So many questions but not one answer. I felt betrayed, angry, abandoned, alone and devastated, all at once. There were emotions flowing through my body at a hundred miles an hour. I slowly and shakily made my way up the stairs and onto my bed.

There was still a lot of time left for them to be away since they were going to be away for a total of three weeks. After that eighth night, I never heard from Anna or the children, nor from Lucy. They had been in a foreign country and no contact was being forged. I also knew that there wasn't any way of contacting them either because of the phone situation. Due to my legal status, I was also unable to travel to them. My hands were tied, I had never felt so helpless in my entire life.

The days that followed were torturous. I could not eat nor sleep. I stayed home from work and was unable to accomplish anything around the house. I was broken and only my family would have provided the cure I needed. It seemed that every hour of every day and of each night, I'd run down the stairs to the basement and ask Richard and Daniel if they had heard anything from anyone. They'd always reply to me with a "No." They were very short in their answers and blew me off. They appeared to have known more than they were letting on; they were ignorant and stupid in a casual yet menacing way. I asked myself, "What is going on?" I didn't have any problems nor misunderstandings with them before but they were treating me like a total stranger.

I tried providing myself with reasons and explanations of what took place during that phone call. I entertained ideas of excuses to convince myself that everything would be fine although a little corner in my mind knew that things were not right. Something had definitely gone wrong. It was very difficult for me to entertain an idea of something happening to my family, so I'd be stuck there totally helpless. There were so many things, so much evidence, to the ideas that were occurring, yet still, I refused to come to terms with them. Maybe I was afraid to face a reality that the truth was more painful than it seemed. My dreams and the suspicions and eerie, nagging voices all grew stronger and more terrifying. I could neither understand nor conclude what was happening. I began missing Kevin, Linda, and Anna to the point I was going out of my mind. I couldn't function, I couldn't do anything without a constant tapping in my heart that something was wrong. I simply refused to come to terms with it.

On the eve of the night Anna and the kids were to return, I was sitting on the floor of the family room in a corner when the door in the kitchen that led to the basement made a knocking sound. I quickly sprouted up, ran to the kitchen, and opened the door. It was Daniel, Anna's brother, who said that he had a message for me. Daniel told me that Anna had called earlier and told him to tell me that if I wanted, it was totally up to me to pick them up at the airport, that they'd be arriving as originally scheduled, if not they'd find their own way home. The message was so cold and I felt every extent of it. The message was a total shock to me because I knew then that something was definitely wrong. Anna was the total opposite of the person who left that message. The Anna I knew wouldn't have a reason to leave a message with someone else, but would have told me directly.

The coldness that emanated from the message could never have indicated to me what I should have prepared myself for the following day. Although things weren't where they were supposed to be, I still believed that once they returned, everything would be explained and we'd return to living our all so perfect lives. Little did I know that this was the beginning and I did not have a clue about the magnitude of the storm that was going to thunder upon me. The life Anna and I lived prior to them making that trip was a fairy tale, but now, was about to be completely and undeniably different.

Chapter Four

As I lay in bed that night, the leering eyes and whispering voices had returned. This time I wasn't as scared as I was the previous nights. I had begun to have a sickening immunity to the fear-driven whispers. I attempted to telepathically communicate with the voices as I hid beneath the blankets, afraid of confrontation. I could not have translated the voices due to the number of whispers simultaneously attempting to speak. The voices grew louder but not to the audibility of speech. They were still at a whisper but that of a more aggressive nature. As my arms rested beside me, I tenderly pinched the blanket and slowly pulled the sheet that covered my face, barely exposing the edge of my right eye where I could hardly decipher an image. The leering eyes were in abundance, I could now see them clearly. There were hundreds of pairs, if not thousands. As I stared into the right corner of the ceiling, peeking through the tiny space between my index and middle fingers, I observed a very specific set of eyes that seemed familiar. There was a warmth to them, a compassionate look that caught the contact of my stare, beautiful and brown, big and bold, and strangely comforting. As the provocation of the voices continued, the compassionate pair began to cry. There were tears on the wall, slowly making its created and unplanned journey to the floor. It was continuous and plentiful but thin and clear. I was now scared and my heart skipped many beats. The voices then stopped and the hundreds, if not thousands, of eyes disappeared except for that passionate pair. They were not scary, not in the least, but the passion and sorrow of that pair ran a chill through my spine. I questioned the reality of what was there, I questioned my sense of self-awareness; was I awake or was I dreaming? The eyes kept staring at mine and suddenly vanished. They were not gone a minute when I observed the tears flowing to the floor had remained. The eyes may have vanished but the tears had stayed. The walls were now weeping, a remnant of the pair that once was there. It flowed from its origin in the corner of my high ceiling. I could have seen the path it was taking; it ran down the walls like a slow but steady stream, a glittering but crystal-clear liquid that made two separate flows from where those eyes once were.

The shimmer of light that forced its way through my window curtain helped to identify its purity and clarity. As scared as I was, I could not take my eyes off of these weeping walls. The flow had mesmerized me; it was peaceful, calm, slow, gentle, and continuous. It possessed a strength that had a hold on me, that captivated my thoughts. Now the voices returned, not all at once, but as a symphony where they gradually increased their quantity and progression to their climaxing whisper. I noticed the tears on the wall slowly retracting itself to where the eyes once were and the more the voices, the faster the retraction. The voices had become dominant and the tears that had fallen were all gone, they had retracted to whence they had come. It appeared that a battle had taken place and the voices were victorious. They had forced the tears into retreat and the voices had begun to celebrate.

After hours of listening to and fending off the perturbing whispers, I tried pulling the pillow over my head and sticking my fingers into my ear to block out the infuriation. Nothing I tried was working as the whispers became louder and louder and wouldn't allow me the benefit of rest. I angrily got off the bed and went to the living room area on the first floor and laid on the sofa. I made many attempts to self-explain what was taking place but I couldn't. Growing up in the Caribbean, I had heard of such stories, of things of this nature occurring, but I never believed them, I thought they were just that: stories. I explained them away by forcing myself to believe they were just a reflection of my subconscious.

After a difficult night, I awoke to the sounds of the garbage truck on our local street. I sprung off the sofa and rushed to the bathroom to prepare myself for what I thought would be the best homecoming ever. The hairs on my face had grown very long, it took me a while before I got cleaned up. I got dressed and sat on the sofa, staring at the old but beautiful wall clock, anticipating their return. Time dragged along, the hands on the clock moved in slow motion, even the birds that chirped seemed softer and slower. They had been away for three weeks and my anxiety grew as the hands on the clock made its slow rotations. As the time drew closer, I departed to the airport and parked close to the runway so I could see when the plane landed. My thoughts were distant and I cannot retrace nor recall my journey there, even if I wanted to.

After being there for an hour or so, I finally saw the Boeing 747 gliding in. My eyes stared at it from where it had touched down all the way to the docking gate. Off I went to the arriving terminal to await them. I was standing amidst a crowd looking down the pathway for arriving passengers.

About an hour and a half had passed and many passengers had already begun exiting to meet up with their loved ones. Through each crowd, I would peer through the spaces in their gathering and stand on my toes to look over the heads of others to steal a glance of the forthcoming pathway. There weren't any signs of Anna and the kids. Thoughts of betrayal once again entered my mind and I began to question the validity of their return. Before the thoughts of validity could have digested, I looked up and the moment in which I had waited for, for so long, had finally approached. I saw the four of them from a distance ambling down the pathway that led to where I stood. Anna in the front, the two kids on the sides, and Lucy at the back. Immediately, I felt relieved, I was so happy to see them once again.

Three weeks had seemed like three lifetimes. So much had happened, my world had felt normal again. The awkwardness I had felt earlier in the weeks had somehow faded to non-existence. Now that they were here, I could finally have some answers to what had been plaguing me for such a long time. That feeling of total happiness lasted just a moment though. As they drew closer, the tears that had built up in my eyes slowly started to recede into the glands from which they came. When eye contact was made with Anna, I saw in them a very cold and distant soul. A chill ran through my entire body. It was not Anna. She may have worn the appropriate clothing, owned the distinctive physical features, and had the presence, but I knew it wasn't Anna. I saw through her, but without an explained or justified thought, my brain forced the acceptance that it was Anna.

As they neared me, Anna and her mother never said hi nor hello, not even a whisper. I then asked Anna, "How are you? How was the flight?" I never received an answer. She glared into an unknown direction of nothingness and pretended I wasn't even there. I then took my eyes off of Anna and turned to Kevin and Linda. I knelt onto the concrete flooring, extended my arms, and they rushed toward me. I held onto them while tears streamed down our faces. I didn't understand why they were crying so hysterically. Was it because they were so small and didn't know any better? Or was it because of the sixth sense that children possess? After we held each other for a bit, I got very upset. I did not take notice before, but Kevin and Linda emitted a strange and putrid odor. They smelt as though they had not showered in weeks. When I took a closer look, their clothes were filthy and most horribly, there were mosquito bites all over the exposed parts of their bodies. Their hair was not combed and they looked totally unkept. "Did they even belong to anyone?" I asked myself. I became frustrated with everything. The phone calls that never happened, the sleepless nights, the silence, and my emotions were being tested. My patience grew thin and the ignorance of the situation extended its arms and was tapping me on the shoulder. The patience and understanding within me kept me from a drastic answer to it all. I swallowed the pride, the anger, and digested the hurt for the sake of peace.

I grew angry, grabbed Kevin, and hastily departed to the parking garage, but not before letting Anna know to wait at a certain spot outside the terminal which provided easy access to the loading of their bags. After retrieving the car, I returned to the spot in which I asked them to await my return. There was no one there. I spent about five minutes looking through the North and South curbsides seeking their location, but could not. Taking Kevin along, I left the car parked at the curb and returned inside to look for them. I spent five minutes looking without success until I returned outside. It was about thirty feet to the North of where I parked that my eyes caught sight of them. I got back into the vehicle and told my brother, Stephen, who had accompanied me to the airport, to drive the car up to where they were. Kevin and I walked up to where they were and Stephen pulled up in order to get the bags into the vehicle. Not to any understanding of mine could I guess why they were being so cold. I said nothing out loud but asked myself many questions. Why was I being treated this way? What have I done to deserve this? What in God's name is going on? I just did not understand anything at all. On our way home, I decided to break the silence and ask Anna and Lucy what was wrong. I asked them, "Why are you giving me such a hard time? Why are you being so cold?" I received no response. Every time I asked a question, I would look into the rear-view mirror to where my brother was seated and we'd exchange looks at each other as to suggest, "What's going on?" I knew then, it was finally confirmed, that all the different suspicions I'd had about something being wrong, were all true. I was naïve before but it was now time to investigate and get to the bottom of all this considerable nonsense. The rest of the journey was of total silence, no one said anything.

After arriving at the house, Lucy quickly got out of the car and speedily went through the driveway and into the basement where she lived. The rest of us went inside after unloading the bags. I asked Stephen to stay the night because it was already late, and I would take him home in the morning.

Almost immediately after getting inside, I took the children's clothing off, I actually tore them off. I was furious from the way they smelt and angrily put them into the tub. I doused them completely with the shower hose. There were marks of old and new insect bites all over so I gently scrubbed their entire little bodies, from their heads to their toes, again and again. I then took them out, dressed them in decent clothing and tucked them into their lonely beds. Linda was a bit uneasy and crying a lot so I put her next to Anna on our bed and I returned to Kevin's room where I laid for the rest of the night. It was already very late so I did not bother asking Anna anything. I had already decided that I'd pick it up in the morning. I went to bed knowing that there were many questions that needed answers. The changes in her were too obvious and Anna wasn't Anna. Who she was, I didn't know, but this was not the wonderfully amazing woman that boarded the dreaded flight three weeks ago.

The next morning, as soon as I got out of bed, I went to the master bedroom where I had left Anna and Linda, and to no surprise of mine, they weren't there. I proceeded to the first floor and saw Anna sitting on a chair looking at television. I approached her, knelt to the floor and rested my palms on her knees. Stephen was sleeping very close by, on the sofa, so I didn't want to make much noise. Quietly, I began asking Anna, "What is wrong? What is going on? Why are you so angry with me?" I got no replies. Anna never looked in my direction. She gazed into the television, totally indulged in the pointless sitcom that aired. Her gaze into the screen of oblivion had swallowed her, and to her, I did not exist. Without exaggeration, I'm sure I asked Anna about fifty times, "What's the matter?" I tried asking many different questions, the same question in different ways, from different angles, but still never received a response. I gave up. I told her that if she didn't want to answer any questions, she should just nod her head. She then nodded in approval and I thought to myself that this was the opportunity to get some answers.

The first question I asked was if she had slept with someone else. She nodded as to imply, "No." I breathed a sigh of relief because I thought I would have been able to forgive her for anything else but that. After that question was asked and answered, I then continued asking different questions. I asked many crazy questions but still got the nodded "No" as a response. I realized that she didn't want to talk so I told myself that I should leave her alone before she gets upset. I then told her that I was going to ask one final question. I asked her if anyone knew what was wrong whom I could speak with. Anna finally said, "Yes," verbally. I then asked her, "Who?" She did not answer, but my logical guess was Lucy. When I turned to Anna and asked her if it was her mother, she nodded yes.

I got off my knees and hastily went through the kitchen and into the inside door to the basement. I knocked on the door and asked to come in. From behind the closed door, I heard Lucy's voice murmur, "Yes, sure, come in." She was in the kitchen preparing a meal so I sat on the stairs and asked her if there was anything she could have told me in regards to her daughter about what was taking place. She then maliciously said, with a silly smirk that overwhelmed her hideous face, that she didn't have any idea what I was talking about.

As she continued to dice the items spread across the counter top, I could see bubbles from the pot atop the stove. The smell that came with the steam that was released was one of disgust. She was cooking something very unfamiliar to that of what was commonly known to me. I jokingly asked her, "What the hell are you making?" She slowly turned her head, grinned, and said, "This is what I've been feeding your family for years." I asked her again, "What is that?" She said, "Don't worry about it, get your ass out of here!" Richard, who was sitting on a chair in the living area, walked over and stood at the base of the stairwell. He was there to protect her from me as he thought I would have been agitated from what she had said. He told me to leave. She continued to stir her meal from hell and added the diced vegetables she had prepared. As I made the motion to lift myself from the stairs, Lucy yelled, "Get out! Get out!" Richard gestured with his pointed finger the way to the door. As baffled as I was, I noticed that I wasn't going to get anything out of either of them, so I returned upstairs.

I resumed asking Anna different questions and she continued to nod. I finally asked the right question, or so it had seemed. I asked her if she had found someone else and she nodded yes.

By the time the answer had sunk into my system, I was already heartbroken, but I had to keep my composure. I needed to get as much information as possible. I kept interrogating her, not by choice, but as a cover-up. I kept asking her questions based on what she had told me. The questions that followed were mumbled from my lips. I was hurt, so I possibly asked many nonsensical questions in an attempt to conceal the embarrassment I felt. I asked her if she didn't love me anymore, if she didn't have any feelings left for me. Anna began answering questions promptly and appeared eager to have nothing to do with me anymore. My fear of all time seemed to have become a reality. I did not know how to react; my mind wasn't there anymore. I remained silent and calmly walked away.

Stephen, who had stayed the night, got up off the sofa due to the commotion taking place around him. I knew he was awake but hid that fact. He told me that he was ready to return home. It was a perfect opportunity for me to get away a bit, to release some of the pressure that had built up. It was about 9 o' clock that morning when we left the house. It was an absolutely silent ride to where Stephen lived. There were so many things going through my mind. From where I stood at this point, it was apparent that my life was over. The life Anna and I had built was slowly being crumbled before my eyes.

After arriving at Stephen's residence, I told him to let everyone know that everything was okay and I'd be fine because I'm sure he would have told them what had occurred. At that moment, tears began to flow from my eyes, my lips could not utter a word because of how much I was hurting. Stephen, after seeing and hearing this, became very reluctant to get out of the vehicle. I guessed he was afraid I was going to do something stupid. He kept telling me to come inside and that we'd sit with everyone and talk about it. I refused and somehow managed to convince him that I'd be fine and to let everyone know I'd be okay. Stephen got out of the vehicle and I drove off.

I continued driving without thinking. Where was I driving to? I myself had no clue. I aimlessly drove for miles and miles without a planned route or destination. There were so many things going through my head. I went so far as to consider running the vehicle into a tree or driving over a bridge or into a lake. My life as I once knew it, seemed to have been over. I knew that there wasn't anything good that would come of the situation I was in.

I had unknowingly driven all the way to the beach and decided to park the vehicle and go for a walk. I walked the shoreline at Rockaway Beach for a while and then sat on the sand, just going over things in my head. I began to question myself and often I'd even get a reply out loud. From all the questions and answers, there was one question, however, for the life of me, that I couldn't get an answer to and that question was: "Why, why was all of this happening? Why was Anna treating me like this? Why was she acting the way she was even though she had found someone else? Why not come out in the open and simply tell me about it? Why all the silence? Why all the playing of games?" Those questions kept nagging at me as I did not have the answers. Something strange then happened, I suddenly got up, got into the car and drove off. I was heading home, there was much more taking place than what she was letting on.

On my way there, my elder sister Nancy called. She was very worried. She began telling me that I shouldn't think of doing anything rash or crazy or anything I might regret later. I myself had already made up my mind that I was returning home, so I told her to not worry. When Nancy got off the phone, my mother, Stella, called. She immediately told me to get home and that they were all going to come over.

Upon my arrival at home, I did not go inside but sat on the front step. It had not been ten minutes before my family showed up. My mother, Stephen, Nancy and her husband Ray, my younger sister Drew and her husband Marvin, all approached me. My face was swollen and my eyes were red. They told me I looked awful. My mother and Nancy held my arm and said, "Let's go inside." We opened the door and entered into the living area. Anna was sitting in the same place where I had left her hours before. They were all angry and began interrogating Anna. With all the commotion taking place, Lucy bolted through the kitchen from the basement, after hearing all the fuss, and boldly grabbed a chair to sit beside Anna.

Everyone gathered in the family room. My mom began the questioning with me. I then told her everything, in brief. My family started telling Anna that what she was doing wasn't right. They were telling her that the person she had claimed to have met was probably just using her to come to the United States. Whilst everyone spoke to Anna about the wonderful life we had built, the fantastic kids we were raising, and the great house we just bought, Lucy screamed out, "Leave my daughter alone! What are you people doing?! She found someone else and that is that!" Lucy had put her foot down and she wasn't having any of it.

Throughout everything that was taking place, I realized something. During all the lectures and interrogation, I saw that Anna was completely un-Anna-like. She was so unlike the person whom I had grown to love, respect, and cherish so much. The way in which she acted, way in which she spoke, the words she used, and the tone of her voice were so unlike Anna. The person whom I had adored so much was not there. This person, however, was cold-hearted, arrogant, and rude, unlike the person whom everyone had come to love and respect. I also observed that Anna's mother knew more than what she was letting on. I had asked her earlier that morning and she told me she knew nothing. I knew then, and I know now, that she was the person behind everything. She sat there with a continuous smirk on her face, implying we were all stupid and knew nothing. The look on her face had a confident obliviousness that defeated the questions being asked. The look told a story of guilty confidence and of shameless victory.

My family saw that they weren't getting anywhere. Just then, my brother-in-law, Marvin, decided to take all the men outside, except me of course, because he thought with the situation being what it was, it would have been a better idea for them to be outside. I guess he thought that Anna would probably feel more comfortable and maybe open up a little. After the men went outside, we resumed conversating. Many questions were once again asked to Anna, only this time, Lucy was doing all the answering. She wasn't giving any straight answers either, all questions would be answered in riddles. I observed that as Lucy placed her left arm on Anna's hand, Anna jumped up and screamed, "But I don't love him anymore! I hate him!" I then humbly asked her, "You really don't love me anymore?" Anna quickly replied with a certain and concise "No." Lucy wickedly smiled; Anna had finally given the answer she was hoping for. There wasn't a need to continue the conversation anymore. It all ended abruptly with Anna's answer and Lucy's witty grin. We all saw the deception that they intended for us to see; it was too obvious. Lucy knew we weren't as formidable an opponent to her, her face said it all.

Though obvious, there was a hidden agenda written over her, there was more to it, something which we knew nothing of.

My sister, Nancy, decided to take me upstairs to get some of my clothing. I guess she thought Anna needed some time and space. We grabbed a few pieces of clothing, made our way down the stairs through the desolate living room, out the door without hesitation, and proceeded toward the car. When we all sat in the car and were ready to drive off, Kevin and Linda, who were in the basement playing while everything was taking place, ran outside to the front. They stood in front of the house and put their little hands out and started a slow wave. They both looked so confused as the tears in their eyes fell down their cheeks and their little hands slowly waved. As the car was being driven away, I felt as though someone was slowly pulling my heart from my chest. A sick reality had begun to resonate within me. I had never felt this way before. I was being voluntarily dragged away, if there is something like that, from my family, the one thing that dignified my existence. The car pulled out and we were gone.

In our world, there are things we find ourselves doing that we sometimes cannot explain, but we do them anyway. We realize after the fact that we did them. We question ourselves as to why and how, but we accept we've done them. As a common and mere human being, I tell myself it's just a mistake I've made. It was emotions that played a part in a decision of haste. I have always found an excuse to justify the stupidity of a hasty act. There are things we all cannot explain, this being one of them. Whatever the reasons we commit these stupid and hasty acts, remember, they are not always a mistake, but sometimes a necessity.

Chapter Five

We arrived at Nancy and her husband Ray's house, who lived together with my mom and Stephen. We all gathered in the living area along with Drew and Marvin. We were having an intervention. We all spoke about what had happened and the possibilities that existed to the reasons of why it was happening. Approximately two hours had passed and Drew and Marvin had left to go home. The rest of us remained up for a while, with my mother and sister making every attempt to comfort and console me in every way they could. It was already late in the day and everyone decided to get some rest and to pick everything back up in the morning. While everyone went to their respective rooms, I couldn't sleep. How could I? I stayed up not by choice, but by the emotions that ran through my body that enabled a rise in my adrenaline which forced my mind and body awake. I called my friend, who was also my boss, Carlos, and asked him to use his vehicle. Between Anna and I, we possessed only one vehicle and I left it at the house when we left earlier that afternoon. He did not live very far from where I was located at the time so I walked over, borrowed his keys, and took off back to where Anna and I lived.

I parked in front of the house, sitting there, ogling the front porch. Memories of wonderful past times filled my moments while sitting there. As I stared into the yard, I remembered the moments when I pushed Kevin around on his tricycle. I recalled myself washing the vehicle in the front driveway, I remembered Anna and me taking the groceries in after shopping. There were all these great memories that made themselves available to me without notice. I sat there reminiscing on all that once was and thinking about how they had become now. I thought to myself, "This could not have been the end." Anna and I worked too hard, we were in love too much, our dreams and goals were in unison since the day we met. I was never great alone, neither was she, but together, we were unstoppable. We saw eye to eye in everything we did. I remembered when we visited a fortune teller once, who had said that we were soulmates. Anna and I always believed that and we proved it. Together, we were a force to be reckoned with. Our bond was not typical, it was made in heaven and this little blip in our objectives was not going to stop me from attempting to resolve this unwelcomed storm that had struck. I decided to let everything remain the way they were, for the night only, then drove off. I arrived back at Nancy's where everyone was still asleep. I laid on the sofa in the living room where I stayed up for a while but eventually cried myself to sleep.

Morning came and I was awakened by the aroma of a traditional dish being cooked. It had been a while since I had last eaten my mother's dishes or even smelt the aroma of that "love in the recipe" that she placed so much emphasis on. I went into the kitchen where she stood, still in her pajamas stirring the food in the steel pot. I jumped onto the kitchen counter, gently sat, and braced myself against the refrigerator. My mother asked me how I was holding up and I began telling her about everything that had transpired, leading up to this day. While narrating to her, Nancy had also awakened and joined us in the kitchen, where she keenly listened to what was being said. We all had come to the conclusion that what was taking place was strange. There wasn't any way that this was normal. It was freakishly sudden; it was too coincidental with the spontaneous trip to Guyana that was orchestrated by Lucy. I thought to myself how revealing things can be when thoughts are shared and different opinions are expressed. We remained there and continued talking while we indulged ourselves in very tasty and reminiscing bites of my mother's fantastic old school meal. I told mom and Nancy that I needed to go back. I needed to go home and attempt to sort things out with Anna. They agreed with me so I left them in the kitchen and I proceeded to the shower. Shortly after, I emerged and said goodbye to mom and Nancy.

I returned home and everything appeared normal. As I entered through the front door, Anna was sitting in the living area, holding Linda as she slept. Kevin was nowhere to be seen. I assumed he was in the basement as he couldn't have been anywhere else. I asked Anna if she was okay and to my surprise, she replied with a "Yeah." I asked her to talk, just the both of us, no intrusion of anyone. She agreed and we proceeded upstairs where she laid Linda to rest in her crib. We entered the master bedroom and sat on the edge of the bed. We began talking and to my amazement, Anna was very polite and sincere. She was the old Anna. The look in her eyes was what I remembered it to be; her body language and her gestures all seemed to have been restored. Anna began telling me that she did not know what was occurring with herself. She said that she loved me but something inside her was overpowering her thoughts and actions and she had no control of it. She told me there was no one else and she couldn't understand what was happening. She continued to tell me that she'd feel one way now, but a different way a little while after that. One minute she'd be totally in love with me and the next, she'd totally despise me. She was caught in the middle of a tug of war and had no control of which end to pull for. Her thoughts appeared confusing to me but, strangely enough, I was actually understanding what she meant. The words she spoke made me feel relieved. Anna and her mother were extremely close and now that I had this opportunity to reveal what I had thought about Lucy's involvement, I was going to let her know.

I asked Anna what happened in Guyana. She said that she couldn't remember most of her time spent there. There were bits and pieces that she did remember but they weren't clear. She remembered being at the beach with Lucy and other strangers and that they were performing a type of ceremony that she didn't have any knowledge of. Before Anna could have continued, a shout came from the floor below. It was Lucy calling for her. "Anna! Anna!" was shouted loudly from the speaker of a mouth from the first floor. Anna replied, "I'll be right there!" I told her to go and that we'd finish the conversation later. She said, "Okay," and proceeded to where Lucy had called. I followed her down the stairs and saw Lucy standing in the dining room anxiously awaiting her. Lucy looked at me with such disgust – her face swelled, her teeth clenched, and she hastily retreated to the basement along with Anna. While the door was open, Kevin ran through and shouted, "Daddy! Daddy!" and ran toward me. I grabbed onto him and held him so tightly, giving him many hugs and kisses. I sat down on the sofa and was overlooking all of the insect bites on his body. Some were drying and others appeared to have dried completely, but little fainted scars had remained. Kevin made his way to the floor and sat next to the entertainment unit at the base of the stairs that led to the second floor, where he played with his toy truck.

I sat there replaying everything in my mind. My thoughts were filled with the intention of getting Lucy out of the house. I knew this would be a challenge due to the fact that it's New York and eviction laws were not as simple as other states. Anna's mother would have made it hard as well but I knew she was behind everything and for me to stand a chance, I needed her out. It was imperative to get Anna on my side and to make her understand, to make her truly believe it was her mother behind everything.

As I sat there contemplating with my own thoughts, Lucy made her way up the stairs and into the living area. My thoughts immediately stopped. Her presence demanded full attention. I looked at her and she returned my look with her own stare. There was an evil look on her face; a cruel intention brewed in her eyes and she immediately knew I was a problem for her. She knew because I would not take my eyes off of her. We had entered into this staring contest and neither of us wanted to back off. My eyes would not allow her the victory over me. As the evil staring contest continued, Kevin was on all fours making his way up the stairs. Lucy added to her stare. She had made a sudden wicked and nasty smirk at me. Her face lit up as she turned around and proceeded to where Kevin continued to ascend. She slowly walked up the stairs while continuing her wicked and obscured smirk, viciously grabbed Kevin by his left arm, and began to pull him down the stairs, tread by tread. His little body was being bounced from stair to stair in slow-motion while she grinned at me. I was still sitting on the sofa, I couldn't move. My brain was telling me to move but my body refused to take action. I looked on to what this crazy woman was doing with my son and I couldn't do anything. I was being forcefully held down by an invisible force that mentally incapacitated my ability to control my physical motions. As she made her way down the stairs with Kevin harshly bumping from one tread to the other, screaming and yelling, "Daddy! Daddy!" I couldn't move. He attempted to free himself of her tightly held grasp but she was too strong for him. I was being held onto the sofa by a force beyond my comprehension. I could feel every stair that touched his skin and I felt his every cry. I swallowed deeply and yet couldn't break through the force holding me on the sofa. Lucy finally stopped, just about two treads from the bottom, looked at me, wickedly grinned and slowly said, with so much conviction, "Don't matter what you do or what you try, they will never, ever come back to you." I was enraged and my brain was overpowered by the telepathic hold of Lucy. I had never witnessed anything like that before. She had revealed to me an example of the power that was available to her. It was a warning to me and her message was received with total attentiveness. She then completed her slow and treacherous journey with Kevin and dragged him as he cried his way to the basement. The door was slammed shut and I was again able to move.

I was in a sense of shock. I did not know what had just happened. This was the most vulnerable I had ever been. I knew then that I was up against something more powerful than I had imagined. I may have won the staring contest but she may have allowed me to. She wanted to show me just how vulnerable and pathetic I was to her. Those words that she said resonated within me, they became a part of me. They made me feel weak and broken. I knew now that I had surrendered, that I had miserably lost. The hope, which I had earlier, had vanished. Lucy's words took everything from me. The little strength I had mustered, the glimmer of hopefulness I had gained earlier, and the light I had allowed in were all disintegrated by one set of spoken words and a demonstration of an inhuman power. I knew Lucy had help and that she was using more than just her physical strength and wit to keep me suppressed. I knew because I had witnessed it.

Anna made her way up from the basement, went to Linda's room, took her out of her crib, walked past me, and retreated back to the basement. For the remainder of that already eventful day, I sat around the house doing nothing. I was withdrawn, lost in my own emotions, and felt defeated. I asked myself, "How am I to win a battle where I don't possess control over my own abilities?" I couldn't find an answer nor could I have accepted defeat. I was too stubborn and would not allow Lucy the happiness nor satisfaction of my apparent surrender. I paced the living room from the stairwell to the front door while the thoughts of Lucy's prior actions completely overtook me. I became drained by the thoughts of my trouncing that I had sustained from Lucy. I left to the upstairs bedroom and threw my evidently useless mind and body to the bed.

My purposeless thoughts were interrupted by the ringing of my phone. It was Carlos, my boss. He wanted to know when I was returning to work. I needed the money, *we* needed the money, so I told him I would return the next day. We set a time and then hung up the phone.

Later that afternoon, while I prepared my uniform for work, Anna returned upstairs along with Kevin and Linda. She appeared different, her eyes were withdrawn and did not acknowledge me sitting on the sofa. I thought to myself, "Here we go again." She took the kids to the shower where I then followed. We both participated in the bathing and dressing of the kids and then laid them down to sleep. During this time, Anna and I were able to exchange a few words with each other. Even though very few were spoken, she appeared to have slowly emerged to being Anna again, the Anna whom I spent time with earlier that morning. I saw my opportunity again and didn't waste time. I immediately began telling her everything, from my perspective. I told her what Lucy had done to Kevin and the effect it had on me. She began telling me everything from her viewpoint and we both were on the same page. We were now seeing eye to eye and were able to finally talk. I told her how much I loved her and the kids and asked her why she was allowing Lucy to control her life. She told me that Lucy had total control of her and she wasn't sure how to release herself from her grasp. I explained to her that she needed to stay away from the basement and Lucy and that we'd work on getting them to move out. We went down the stairs and into the kitchen to where the door that led to the basement was closed. We braced the breakfast table and chairs tightly against the door, ensuring that it could not have been penetrated from the other side, then returned upstairs. I started to feel relieved as if everything would work itself out. The kids were lying comfortably in their beds, fast asleep, and Anna and I were united again. Before turning in for the night, Anna and I discussed our plans moving forward. An understanding was reached that she nor the kids would venture into the basement, voluntarily or involuntarily. I mentioned to her I was working the next day and it was imperative for her to stay within her confines and not allow Lucy to enter our space in the house nor allow the kids in the basement. It was after one o' clock in the morning when we realized it was time for me to start heading out to work and her, to bed.

Chapter Six

My job was in transportation and I started very early in the morning when I worked. I needed to pick up my passenger van that was at Carlos's house and drop off his car that I had borrowed. I jumped into the shower and quickly got dressed. I reminded Anna, before I left, what we had spoken about. I then went to Carlos's house, got the van, radioed in to dispatch, and was on my way after receiving an assignment. During the day, I was happy. I kept looking into the future. I was silently planning in my head the ways Anna and I were going to distance ourselves from Lucy. I was slowly regaining my confidence and my sense of self. That feeling of control had returned. I was being empowered by the ideas that I entertained. I worked an entire day and it felt good. I had accomplished something which I hadn't done in a while.

Around two o'clock that afternoon, at the end of my shift, I arrived home, parked the van in front of the house, and entered the house through the front door. As my eyes made its way through the inside, I could see from where I was standing that the table and chairs that had blocked the basement door were removed. The set had returned to its origination at the center of the kitchen. I once again felt defeated. The little headway I thought I had achieved in the past day was immediately taken away and I became very angry. I stood at the basement door and I yelled for Anna and the kids behind the locked doors. I could hear Kevin shouting on the other side, "Daddy! Daddy!" but no one else there was answering. I could hear him climbing the stairs and someone pulling him back down. I could hear his screams, his cries for help. I could hear Linda crying in the faded background. She was too small to understand but not too small to possess the telepathic ability from her brother's bondage. She knew he was being hurt and she cried for him. She cried because he was her flesh and blood and her sixth sense automatically kicked in.

They refused to open the door. As I stood on the other side, kicking and pounding against the stubborn and sturdy door, I pleaded with the deaf ears to leave him alone. I pleaded with them to let the innocent child be free of their desire to keep me away. As I slowly moved away from the door, my screaming son's painful yell gradually vanished. I did not want them to hurt him anymore so I backed off. I cowardly retreated to the confines of the living room, which had become my sanctuary for the past few weeks. The bedroom had become very unsettling to have a comfortable night's rest and the living area provided peace and quiet. There was an emotional turmoil within me. Within short periods of time I would experience happiness and accomplishment, but then it would all be taken away in an instant. The back and forth of my multifarious feelings were breaking me. They were getting to me, and each time I made attempts to overcome them, I would be drawn back into defeat.

As I sat there alone pondering through the events that had taken place in the past few weeks, the doorbell rang and a loud knock immediately followed. I approached the door and through the peephole, I could see the uniformed officers standing on the front porch. Someone had called the police. I let them in and asked if everything was okay. They said someone had called 911 because they were being threatened by someone on the first floor of this house. I attempted to explain the situation and the officers simply told me I needed to take the matter to family court and that I couldn't threaten anyone. I pleaded with them to understand that I was telling the truth. The officers did not believe me nor wanted to listen to me. They went to the back door to the basement and announced themselves.

The basement door opened and Lucy emerged crying. She told them that I was drunk and I became violent. She told them I was pounding and kicking the door because she had taken the kids and my wife into the basement since she was unsure of my intentions. I made attempts to explain to the officers what had really happened but they weren't hearing any of it. They believed her over me. She had convinced them that she was a victim, a victim of my intended abuse, which never happened. Her conniving ways had seduced the officers into a false perception of what transpired. There was nothing I could have done and retreated to the living room. The officers came to me and offered a stern warning. If they were called again, I would be arrested. They asked me if I understood and I nodded to them that I did. They then left and I sat there in disbelief and shook my head.

The basement door unlocked and Anna came through the kitchen and sat next to me. Her eyes were filled with tears, her cheeks were swollen and red, her clothing emitted a rancid odor, and she appeared distraught. She simply asked me to leave them alone. She quietly pleaded with me to not mess with them. She asked me to stay away from Lucy, that I didn't know who I was messing with. I wasn't sure if she asked me to stay away because she wanted me to, or because she was trying to protect me. I asked her what she was afraid of and she replied, "Nothing." The whirlwind of what was happening was too recurrent. I asked Anna what happened to all we had discussed the night before, about the plans for the kids. She said that she didn't know what I was talking about, got up, and went into the basement. I was appalled and upset by the fact that what we had spoken about was all for nothing.

I was working the next day so I took a shower and went to bed. While lying in my room, a room that had become a constant awakening for intentions of cruelty, I pulled the blankets over my head and attempted to sleep. As I progressed into the brink of sleep, the whispering voices had returned. I again became very scared. The voices were in abundance once more. I kept the blanket tucked under the edges of my entire body. I was afraid to take a peek. I was afraid of what my wandering eyes would see. I had become fully awakened by the voices that had once again increased their heightened murmur. In an attempt to overcome my fear, I slowly retracted the blanket that covered my head to reveal the corner of my right eye. As I carefully and systematically opened my eye, I was greeted by the sight of the passionate pair in the right corner of the ceiling. Those passionate brown pair of eyes had materialized again. I remembered the first time I saw those eyes and I was not frightened. I tried recognizing the pair as they seemed so familiar but they were too faint. They were too distant and appeared only as a blurred silhouette. While the voices continued with their speechless and wordless whispers, the eyes would ogle in my direction. It's as though they were warning me, as if they were there looking over me. I assumed the best from them because they gave me comfort and I was not threatened by them. I remembered they had gotten rid of the voices before and it was the voices that scared me. It was the voices that brought out the fright, hatred, and anger in me.

As I paid a closer look at the fainted and silhouetted pair of eyes, I noticed that they had begun to weep and I started to feel its sorrow. I felt a connection with the tears that flowed. I asked myself if the tears were a reflection of things to come or a reflection of things that passed. I did not know the answer but I felt connected to the tears in some weird and comforting way. As the tears flowed freely along its created path on the walls, I realized the voices started to decrease. As the tears flowed more rapidly, the voices were audibly becoming more and more silent and my fears subsided. The walls were once again weeping. The pair of eyes had remained and the glittering of the tears had taken over control of the room. The incomprehensible voices and the scare that they brought with them had now disappeared and the departure of the compassionate pair of eyes followed short after. Now that the eyes were gone, the tears had remained. The walls continued its weeping and it gave me comfort. It gave me peace. I had become drawn to the tears and knew that they were there for my protection and guidance. It had defeated the voices that were harmful and I began to trust that the passionate pair was there as a warning or as support, I couldn't decipher which. There were many things that had happened previously and I knew there was much more ahead. I had fallen into a peaceful trance while staring at those weeping walls and didn't know when I fell asleep.

I woke up at 1 o' clock in the morning by the alarm I had set and I still remembered everything. I knew that I was not alone and was determined to fight. I now had a companion in my miseries and was willing to do anything to rescue my family from this evil woman. With total enthusiasm, I flew off the bed, got dressed, and out the doors I went.

Chapter Seven

A t work that day, I concocted various ideas, various plans, to get Anna and the kids out – I needed to. I played with different scenarios in my head. I needed to talk to someone so I called my mother and Nancy to seek their permission for a visit with them. They agreed to meet with me that afternoon. I finished work at approximately two o' clock that afternoon and drove over to mom's house.

Nancy came home from work that day around three o' clock and we sat in their living room where I began to tell them all that was taking place. They offered little advice and little suggestions but they made it seem clear that Lucy was the one to be blamed. They strongly suggested that she was involved with voodoo and I laughed at the thought. Some people call it different things; voodoo, obeah, black magic, and witchcraft are only some of the common names. I was ignorant to the existence of a myth that had been around for generations. Maybe I was naïve but I did not want to believe that a mere human, even someone as evil-minded as Lucy, could have had any association with a cult of evil believed to have existed only in stories that our ancestors told, a cult of evil that involved summoning of the dead and taking control of others through the use of spiritual beliefs and connotations. I had heard stories from friends and family who claimed they were victims of such deeds but I still failed to believe that my situation had any involvement of such a mythical evil. With Lucy, it was different. She appeared to have been the devil herself. It's as though the devil had manifested himself into her as a cover up to conduct his evil ways. She was too crude and mercilessly effective to be that of a human.

My mom, Nancy, and I spoke for a long while about stories they had heard, stories that involved spiritual summoning, possessions, and various forms of evil spirits that may have played a part in the family's history. These stories were a revelation to me as I had not heard or seen anything that ever gave me any inclination that such forces actually existed. Growing up in New York possibly spared me the unwanted knowledge of the way of life in Trinidad. We spoke for a while and I decided to return home, now armed with a little more knowledge than I had in the morning. I was somewhat confident and had a regained sense of enthusiasm to take control of my situation and bring Anna and the kids back to me.

As I returned home, while pulling into the front of the house, I observed Anna's father, Richard, and her brother, Sam, sitting on the front step. I parked, stepped out of the vehicle, and approached the front of the house and the stairs where they sat. They were sitting side by side and blocked the entrance to the doorway. I greeted both of them and they returned the gesture. There were a set of five treads, made of brick and mortar, that made up the front entryway to the house. The treads were just about four feet in width and were boxed in with steel railings on each side. They sat on the uppermost tread and left no space for me to get through. As I made my way up the stairs, I expected that they would shift to either side or even get up and make a path to the doorway for me but they did not move. They did not flinch a muscle. I asked for their excuse and they told me, "You're not going in." I asked, "What the fuck is wrong with you people? Are you people out of your fucking minds or something? This is my freaking house and you cannot stop me from getting in!"

Standing on the lowest tread of the step, looking up to them, I reached into my pocket and pulled the keys out. I was determined. Adrenaline had built up within me and I was making sure to get into the house. At this time, Lucy had reached around to the front of the house on the driveway side. She yelled, "Hey you! What do you think you're doing? Get lost from here!" I looked at her and said, "Why don't you just shut the fuck up and get lost, you old hag!" To my surprise, she didn't move, she actually stood there and grinned. I had somehow managed to compose myself for a few seconds and was able to call my mother. She heard what was taking place in the background and told me she was on her way. Before hanging up, she told me to not do anything stupid. She said they were trying to provoke me and no matter what, I should keep calm. I put the phone back into my pocket and the argument resumed.

Chapter Eight

We lived in a quiet and family-oriented community in Queens. All the families that lived there had known each other and were all friendly. There were always mutual greetings of friendship when the paths of each other were crossed. We assisted each other with the kids while playing on the streets, with the taking in of groceries, and the taking out of trash.

While the argument resumed, all of the neighbors were outside their respective houses, some on the street, some on their front porch, and others peeped through the blinds of their front windows. There were many yells and curses that went back and forth between Lucy, Richard, Daniel, and I. Anna and the kids were nowhere to be seen. I assumed they were tucked away in the basement and unaware of what was taking place on the outside. The basement was quite secluded and very well insulated so they may not have been aware of what was transpiring just beyond the outside of those walls. The exchange of unpleasantries continued to escalate with every passing second. I made my way up another tread with full determination and anger to get past them. As I made my move, so did they. They both stood up with their chests pushed out and told me in unison to back off. Lucy was shouting and she said, "Cuff him, cuff the fool!" as she wickedly grinned. I made my way up another tread and that's when Daniel swung his clenched fist at me. I evaded his punch and jumped back to the concrete landing. I was enraged as Lucy kept screaming and telling them to hit me.

They made their trek down the stairs and, without thinking, I unbuckled my broad leather belt that I wore on a daily basis. I wrapped two rounds around my right wrist and began to flail it at everyone. Daniel and Richard were attempting to subdue me while throwing their inadequate punches. I failed to give them the opportunity for victory as I avoided their untimely advancements. Lucy came closer, she wasn't afraid, she was actually smiling. As the buckle made its impactful contact across the various parts of their bodies, she continued to grin. I was flailing the belt as hard as I could. As frustration was released, I felt good. I was getting payback for all they had done to me. I continuously flailed the belt at them and they could not overpower me. My adrenaline had taken over and I was unstoppable. They never had an opportunity to lay a hand on me. Lucy, while taking a beating, just stood there as the buckle crossed her cheek and created an immediate tear and a slow flow of blood that trickled down the side of her grinning mouth. She continued to laugh and said, "Now I've got you right where I want you." Daniel and Richard had taken a beating and they were standing to the side. Their faces were gleaming with spots of blood and their clothing was torn from the damage of the buckle, but they had withdrawn. It baffled me how an elderly woman could take a beating as such yet urge me to continue with a smile. Again, I thought she must have been the devil herself.

I finally stopped but Lucy urged me to continue, she was not done yet. She asked me to hit her. I could hear the neighbors yelling, "What the hell is wrong with you? Stop! Stop!" You're hurting them!" I turned to them and said, "Do you all want some of this too?" I was enraged, I went mad. I had released the frustration that had built up for weeks and I was happy about it. I too began to laugh. I was loud and my laughter rid me of the ridicule of my earlier defeats. Lucy had now stopped and she sat on the stairs while I laughed. With all the noise and commotion within the vicinity, someone had called the police. They pulled up, ran into the front yard, grabbed me, and pulled me to the side. They pinned me against the front wall of the house and commanded me to calm down. Lucy then retracted to the corner of the stairs, laid her head pretentiously against the steel railing, and began crying. She was putting on a show. She was acting out in the presence of the unknowing police officers. She wanted to make sure that they understood the pain and suffering I had inflicted upon her, Daniel, and Richard. I had now calmed down and realized that she willfully and sinfully provoked my attack to get me out of the way. I had fallen into her trap and was seduced into a violent act of her own self-preservation. Sam and Richard, who stood at the side of the house toward the front, seemed confused. They appeared to have not known what had just taken place. They looked at me with so much hate. I could see their eyes of vengeance as they pointed their fingers in warning. I urged them to come, I urged them even though the officers were there. I had become lost in the moment that was taking place. I needed a release from the buildup of frustration and anger that was burning within me. They wouldn't come, they would not approach the madman in me that stood in front of them. They were afraid and I did not lay the blame on them for being as timid, as I knew, I myself, was afraid of me.

Lucy would steal glimpses at me across the roadway when no one else was looking and wickedly grin at me. She knew she had won and there was nothing I could now do to avert her insidious plans, whatever they may have been.

By this time, my entire family pulled up and gathered around me and the officer who was guarding me. They tried telling him what was taking place but it was of no avail. My mother had warned me not to be provoked and not to do anything stupid but I did everything to contradict the advice given.

As the officers completed their minor questioning of the parties involved, they walked over to me and advised me that they were placing me under arrest. All of my family's conversations and pleas with them made no difference, they were not hearing it. The officer simply told me that they were placing me under arrest because I didn't have a scratch on my body nor clothing and the others were bleeding with their clothing tattered and torn. I understood and he placed me into handcuffs and seated me into the back of his patrol car.

The neighbors had now retreated to their homes and Lucy, Daniel, and Richard went inside through the front doors of my house. I looked through the windows from the rear seat of the patrol car and smiled. I saw that they had won. I saw that they were now the royalty of my castle and they entered through the doorways of their deserved victory. As they closed the heavy and rugged door behind them, I put my head down onto the car's glass window and cried. The officers got into the car and we drove off. My family stood there helpless as they waved a cautious goodbye.

On our way to the police station, I kept thinking of what I had done and knew that Lucy had entrapped me. I understood what my mother was trying to tell me and it was now too late to reverse the outcome. I wondered if my mother and the others had now hated me for the sinful acts I had committed. I had transformed into an unstoppable beast that was punishing the innocence of humanity. Whether I was coerced into doing so or not, the act was committed and I should have been strong enough to defend against my will for revenge. I had once again built a momentum to regain my family but Lucy was one step ahead as usual. It's as though she knew my moves before I did and she calculated for them. She undoubtedly implemented her deceitful plans and accurately anticipated my reactions.

Chapter Nine

W e arrived in the holding area at the county jail where I was placed into a small cell by myself. I was tired. I had been up since early in the morning and I had exerted all of my energy, all my adrenaline, during an uncalculated fight that I embarrassingly lost. I now had time to reflect on the ridiculous mistake I had made. I dwelled on the idea that my family may now hate me due to how insane I had gotten. I thought about Anna and the kids. I did not know where they were or what Lucy had done with them. During the confrontation, I had not seen them. I didn't know if they were even there. I kept asking myself, "Why is Lucy doing this? Why does she hate me so much now after all those years of getting along?"

An officer approached the cell, opened it, and escorted me to have my fingerprints and mugshot taken. I felt like a criminal. I had no idea how I was going to get out as I was unfamiliar with the law and was unaware of the processes involved. After having my fingerprints and photo taken, I was escorted to a much larger cell where there were a lot of men being kept. The officer told me this is where I was going to remain until the next morning before I could see the judge. He said I would be assigned legal counsel and they would meet me sometime before seeing the judge. Upon entering the filthy cell, I prematurely profiled the people in there. There was a mixture of various ethnicities that were being held on various charges before they could have seen a judge. There was a single and open toilet that emanated a stench that filled the entire area. There were guys with filthy clothing and bloody faces, drunks, and the homeless all thrown into one cell. I ripped my shirt in order to appear tougher than I looked so that no one would get any ideas of bothering me. I found a small clearing close to a wall and sat next to a man who lay asleep while leaned up against a filthy and padded pole. I could not sleep, I dared not. The company which I now kept would not allow me the decency of rest. I forced myself awake and my thoughts of the day filled my time and kept me company. I was completely broken and my enemies were fortified by my stupidity as I sat there in desolation.

Lucy possessed a rare gift rather a rare curse. She had a unique, although evil, ability to demand control. To make things worse, she was unforgiving and cunning. She was able to twist the truths and deliver onto me certain helplessness that would force my inner strengths into submission.

Hours that seemed like days had passed while I sat there drowning in my thoughts. My hands were tied. Suddenly, a voice shouted out my name, "Mr. Woods! Mr. Woods!" I jumped up and made my way to the bars of the cell located on the other end and saw a gentleman standing there, dressed in a cheap, blue suit and tie, carrying a stack of papers in his hand. I approached him and said, "I am David Woods." He had an officer unlock the door of the cell and allowed me to follow him to an office with a small table and three chairs, just outside where I was held. The small, windowless room was ideally reflective of the conundrum I was in. We got seated and he told me that he was a legal aid and he was assigned to me by the court. He explained the process of the legal system to me and told me that I was going to get my proverbial "day in court." We then made our way through a few hallways and a few double doors until we finally emerged into a large hall. I had now noticed it was morning. The sunlight beamed through the upper windows of the hall as I walked through it with my legal aid. We approached a courtroom where he and I waited to be called. When my name was called, we approached a desk positioned just in front of the judge who was perched in his Godly chair. He called my name and my legal aid approached his bench and left me standing before the smaller desk. They did not speak for more than two minutes when he returned and said that I was being "ROR." I did not know at the time what this meant but later found out it meant "Released on Own Recognizance." The lawyer, my hero, had argued that this was my first offense and I would be released with the provision I would return for my hearing dates set by the court. If I did not, a warrant would be issued for my arrest. I thanked the assigned lawyer and made my way to the exit.

As I made my way down the wide front stairs of the huge courthouse, I saw my brother-in-law, Marvin, my sister, Drew, and my mother, Stella. They had made their way to the courthouse because they were given the information by the officers from the night before. I was extremely tired and embarrassed and wanted to be out of there. I silently stood there with my head down, eyes peeled to the floor, and shook my head in absolute discontent. They slowly walked me over to where the car was parked and we departed to Nancy's.

We arrived at Nancy's a short time after and we all gathered in the living area. I was extremely tired and they pulled out the sofa bed where I lay my head to rest. I slept the entire day and half the night. I was awakened by my mother because she knew I had not eaten anything and I must have been hungry. After waking, strangely, I was not hungry but very, very thirsty. I had an uncanny craving for milk. I asked Stella to pour me a glass of milk and she graciously did. After gulping down the filled glass, I asked for another and then another and then another. I had consumed about four glasses of milk when my mom told me to stop. I began to hysterically laugh, a laugh that was unearthly, as told by Nancy.

The events in the following two weeks were what was told to me because I did not remember much. Nancy and Stella later narrated to me what took place over that period of time because I had asked. I wanted to know what happened because what I did remember was unsettling. The first thing I recalled was my brother, Stephen, lying next to me when I opened my eyes. My mother sat next to me on the sofa bed and Nancy sat at the foot of the bed. They appeared to be so happy. It was as though they were seeing me for the first time and they embraced the idea of me opening my eyes with recognition of them all.

Chapter Ten

After arriving at Nancy's, I fell into an elongated sleep. I had slept for two and a half days. After waking, I began to speak in a different tongue. I was uttering words of an unknown language to my family. We would all find out later that it was Urdu, a language of our ancestors, a language that was associated with the long era of Indian and Pakistani history. Nancy and my mother sought help for me. They visited many different houses of worship. They sought advice from friends and relatives, home and abroad. They wanted to know what was taking place with me. They were uneducated but not oblivious towards what they were witnessing. Nancy told me about four days into my unsettling trance that they had invited a couple of religious friends of the Christian religion to pray for me, to sit with them and recite words of the Lord to ward off the evil that had appeared to have taken over my body. She said that I opened my eyes not long into their prayer. As they recited the words of the Bible, I recited along with them. I did not have the Bible in front of me but I knew the words as though from memory or as if I was reading from a text in front of me. They were appalled and kept reciting louder and louder. As they increased their loudness, so would I. Nancy told me that I would wickedly laugh louder and louder while I chimed in from time to time with their recital. I had grabbed a hold of the strange woman's hand and with my index finger, drew a cross on her arm while I continued to recite the holy words of the Bible. She was frightened so she immediately pulled her arm away and ran outside screaming. The family looked on in disbelief as they did not know what was done. The evil that resided within me had protracted itself into the open. I was a force to be reckoned with. The strange woman never returned. She had vacated the premises after being scared off by a power stronger than her mind could comprehend. I became agitated with the recitals and began cursing at everyone in the room. I waved my hands into the air and continued the rants in Urdu. My brother, Stephen, tried holding me down to calm my spirits but I was too strong for him. I pushed him aside like an object of non-existence. His strength was of no match to mine and I treated him as such. I finally ended the chants and fell into a deep sleep once again.

Stella and Nancy had given the responsibility to Stephen to watch over me while I laid in bed. They knew that I needed help beyond which they could provide. Marvin and Drew had known people associated with the church and reached out to them for assistance. They recommended a person in Brooklyn, New York, a person who was said to have communicated with various spirits and rid them of possessions. Nancy and my mother set an appointment and they needed for me to go along with them.

Nancy said they tricked me into going that Saturday and we journeyed to Brooklyn, New York to meet with the priest. Upon entry to the hole-in-the-wall place of a so-called sanctuary from evil, I could smell the lavender and the incense. I peered into the unwelcomed spirit shop and was not very content being there. There was an eerie feeling and it appeared this place was not a sanctuary from evil but one of evil itself. There was an older gentleman there. His wrinkled face and sunken-in eyes traced my every footstep as I made my way to the broken chair where they placed me to sit. This was his profession before he passed on the trade to his son, the person whom we were to meet. I remember the sunken-eyed gentleman walking over to where we waited, looking at me, and saying, "Son, I'm not sure how you are able to bare what you are baring, you shouldn't be alive." Upon hearing this, Nancy and Stella began to cry. They knew that what had a hold on me was more powerful than they had bargained for.

Nancy told me when the old man said that, I got up in repulsion and walked out the front door. Nancy was about to go after me but the old man said, "Don't worry he'll be back, he'll return on his own." He was right. I had returned about thirty minutes after leaving. The sunken-faced man was right, he had not lost his connection from his trade that he practiced for all his life.

Upon returning, the sunken-faced man told everyone else waiting that he was going to put me in front of the line to meet with his son. What he had seen and felt from within me took precedence over the others. His and his son's attention were immediately needed. They weren't happy about it but succumbed to the request anyway. As my turn approached, my mother accompanied me into a secluded room at the back, enclosed by red curtains with a single chair that sat by itself in the center. A young Latino man who was short, chubby, and fair skinned embraced me. He began to chant in Spanish and waved a burning incense in the air while doing so. He opened up a very old manuscript and began to peruse through the dilapidated pages, attempting to find an answer to what was happening. It hadn't been five minutes in this room when his father, the sunken-faced old man, entered to assist. He placed both my hands into the palms of his and recited in Spanish. He did so for about three to four minutes and then let go.

Stella, who was in the room at the time, said what she saw that day would forever be painted in her memory. She said that the sunken-faced old man had chanted verses in an attempt to rid me of the dark spirit within me. What he had not bargained for was the spirit entering into him. She saw and heard the man transform into who she had known as Kali Ma. Kali, in Sanskrit, means she who is black or she who is death. The name, when heard, is associated with destruction. Just the mention of the name brings fear to the people because she was the most destructive Goddess of all. She could be used by common folks for both good and evil. Her followers worship her in order to get their desires fulfilled. Stories were told that a request for Kali Ma would either bring good or evil, but clearly, in this case, it was evident that it was evil. She was the Goddess of death, time, and doomsday who had overwhelmed the old man and was invoked upon me to take my life.

The spirit spoke. The apparent voice of Kali Ma had emerged and with it, came about the anger from her forced conjuring. The son, clearly being out of his expertise, made attempts to question the Goddess. He asked her what she wanted, why she had been invoked upon me, and who had delivered this evil into our realm. As the spirit spoke, it angrily uttered the name "Lucy." She claimed Lucy had made a sacrifice, for a favor on her behalf. Once the sacrifice was made, the spirit did not have any choice but to fulfill the request sought by the conjurer. The spirit and its conjurer had aimed to get me out of the way; they wanted me gone. My mother was frightened as she had never witnessed anything like this before. No one told the old man or his son about Lucy. She wondered if this was a trick but soon realized there was no way that the old man and his son could be aware of Lucy. This, she stated, must have been all too real. There were no other explanations. She was scared and backed up to a secluded corner in the room. Though feeling that way, she positioned herself to bear witness without being noticeable. It was impossible for the older man to mimic Kali because she had too much knowledge of a different culture and language that he had no knowledge of. Stella knew she was witnessing the exposure of a malicious force that had been summoned to take the life of her son. She had heard stories of the revered one known as Kali and was scared to death. There were people whom she had known, back in our country of Trinidad, who worshipped Kali Ma and she had heard of the power associated with her.

The spirit, through the old man, asked for milk. It was thirsty and demanded milk. The son instructed my mom to the refrigerator and she returned holding a half-filled glass of milk with her shaking hand. The milk was slowly being spilled as she neared where the man had stood. The old man, possessed by the spirit, speedily gulped the milk and then was back to being himself. Upon returning to his natural self, the old man told my mother that he could not do anything for us. He said that the spirit was too powerful for him and his son and that we ought to leave. Before leaving, he gave my mom and Nancy a few bottles of lavender and told them to shower me with it. He also gave to them incense sticks to burn. He stated that they should continuously burn the incense sticks because it would prevent the spirit from reemerging.

We returned home and I immediately crawled into the sofa bed where I had made my new home. I was now confined to a bed that was made for seating. The night came and as I lay in bed, in and out of sleep, I would speak out loud with the dreams that transpired from within. While under the influence of what had taken grasp of me, I'd scream out, "Leave him alone! Leave him alone! He's just a child! Take me! Take me!" I would have conversations with myself, appearing to have an argument with someone. I would call out Kevin's name in distress and beg that someone to not hit him, I would plead with the forces within me, "Please don't hit him, he's a child, let him go! Why are you doing this, why?!" The pleading continued for hours and my mom and Stephen would attempt to get through to me, but they couldn't. I was not there with them, physically maybe, but I was apparently fighting a battle elsewhere. Nancy would later tell me that she would sit for hours and listen to what was taking place and she'd attempt to understand the nature of my calls for help but they were only sometimes spoken in English. At other times I spoke Urdu and she couldn't decipher an understandable story from my inner and epic battles. My eyes would remain closed and I would yell and scream and flail my hands into the air but I would not return to the reality of their time. I was being kept in a dream, an evil dream, where it appeared that a battle of life, mine and my son's, was occurring right in front of her eyes. I would scream out, "That is not food, why are you giving him that to eat? Is that shit you're feeding my son? I'm going to kill you, you witch, you witch, you bitch, I'm going to kill you!" My mom knew that Kevin was in trouble. She knew from the projected dreams I was having. She knew that something needed to be done and time was of the essence. As the yelling and the screaming continued for hours, Nancy gathered the others and it was immediately agreed that further assistance was needed. The help that was sought from the old man and his son had aggravated the spirit and it was punishing me for it. The help they thought they had received was not evident. I continued to battle with the forces within me and my family continued to look on. I would embrace myself in defeat, cuddle my knees to my chest, place my hands behind my back, and verbally speak out, "You got me, please let my son go, you got me." The emotions of my otherworldly dream were being acted out in the reality of their world and they watched on in horror. I would then fall asleep within my dream but be continuously asleep in their reality. My mom and the others learned through repetition when I was going into a battling or subdued mode. They had observed me for days and a story was being told through the actions of a dream. They knew I was fighting for the survival of Kevin and they also knew he was my weakness and Lucy was using him to keep me controlled. She was using Kevin to keep me oppressed and under her control.

Ray was a Muslim and he knew of someone in the upper echelon that lived in Trinidad. He was known as a mufti, someone held in high regard within the Muslim circle. They got his number from a mutual friend and immediately called him on the telephone. They spent over an hour explaining what was taking place and the mufti agreed with them that I needed higher help. He said he knew what they were talking about and he had helped people in the past. Nancy and Ray took up a family collection and offered it to the priest to purchase a round trip ticket and pay for his services as well. An agreement was reached and the booking was immediately made.

The mufti, Mudeen, a long-bearded man, arrived the next day. He had a dark complexion and his two-toned beard lay beyond the middle of his neck. There was a cut on his left cheek that had scarred over time. His faded beige pants were shortened to his dry and flaky ankles. As he entered through the living room where I was asleep on the sofa bed, he greeted everyone with "Assalamu-Alaikum," meaning "peace be unto you" in Arabic, and Ray replied,

"Wa-Alaikum-Assalam." He placed his right hand on my head and started praying. He prayed in Arabic and Ray and Nancy joined in. They prayed for about ten minutes before they realized there was no effect on me. Mudeen gathered everyone around and told them to not panic and that he was going to help me. He said that he would be in the room working on getting me better because he had seen this before. They wanted to know what he meant so he began to explain what was taking place. He said that our world, as we know it, is known as a plane. There exists a plane where humans dwell and another where spirits dwell. They were known as jinns. The jinns were evil and they were capable of possession and ultimate destruction. They could only be summoned by someone who has great power and relies heavily on evil beliefs. They explained to him about Lucy and he let them know that he would get to the bottom of it all. He said that while he is in the room, they'd observe different things, weird things, taking place with me. Whilst he continued his unplanned speech, I would open my eyes for short periods of time, look around the room, point my index finger out at everyone, and cruelly smile. He told them to not panic, that it was normal and hopefully it would all be over soon. His intentions, as he attempted to explain, were to capture the jinn and release it to where it had come. While doing so, there was going to be a spiritual battle between him and the jinn inside me. He looked at me, then looked at them, shook his head and said, "He is already very far gone, he is close to dying and I need to begin immediately."

Chapter Eleven

Mudeen made his way to Nancy's room, which was prepped for his arrival. My mom, Nancy, Marvin, Ray, and Stephen were all in shock. They were trying to make sense of what he told them. Even though they knew there was much more to it than what he had explained, they believed him. They were trusting him with my life. They believed he was the answer, my cure, and they placed all hope in him.

As I lay in the bed, I'd blurt out a sentence or two every so often. Sometimes what I said would make sense but other times it wouldn't. As Nancy said, I appeared to be in a continuous deep sleep and I'd be acting out emotions from my dreams that were taking place. The dreams appeared to have been a battle being fought. I wasn't giving up and I battled for my life and my family. They were very much worried about me. I had not eaten in days, my body laid coma-like, and I made no conversations with anyone. My mom knew the sunken-faced man that we had visited in Brooklyn was scared but was truthful. She knew, or they all knew, that Mudeen was up against an unimaginable evil in Kali Ma. They weren't sure what his battle consisted of but they knew that he had to try.

They heard chants coming from the room where Mudeen stayed, they heard his prayers. He was in there for three consecutive days and nights. He had not eaten, nor showered, nor walked. All he did was pray, he prayed continuously. My mom and the others took turns on looking over me and made sure I was never left alone. From time to time they'd hear Mudeen increase the loudness of his prayers and at the same time, they would observe the effect it had on me. I would get agitated, toss and turn, and angrily speak in different tongues. There was a communication taking place from rooms apart, between him and whatever was in me. The prayers recited appeared to have been working, so they had hoped.

Mudeen emerged from the room after three days and told them he did as much as he could have done and it was going to be up to me now to pull through. They looked at him, then me, and saw no difference. They wondered what he had done because there appeared to be no signs of change. They questioned him for information. They were curious and needed to know what had transpired. Reluctantly, he asked everyone to be seated and started to let them know what his prayers had revealed.

He started out by saying that he dug deep within me and within the spirit that had consumed me. Mudeen said that he had seen the likes of Kali Ma before and the destruction she brought. He had not been successful against her before. She had prevailed and he had lost the person he had been assigned to help. Kali Ma would have only been summoned for one reason, and that was death. She was the most formidable power. She had control of other spirits and was feared. She was prayed to as though she was the devil herself, just manifested in a different form.

He revealed to them that Lucy was not Anna's mother. He said all signs pointed to Anna not being born from such evil. He said he understood. He saw with his own being that Lucy had performed an unspeakable act of evil on the island of Guyana. She had brought with her the wrath of that act and sacked it upon me. She was not human. She couldn't have been. She had practiced such evil acts for a very long time and had grown very powerful. The seeds of evil that she sowed had grown on her, it had become a part of her. Mudeen continued to enlighten the family as their ears hungered for more. He told them, "In the battle of good and evil, you cannot believe in the existence of God if you do not accept the existence of the devil." Lucy was the profit of evil; she knew the channels of contact and she knew the summoning power from the old Sanskrit from which she meditated.

Lucy's intentions were clear to him and he explained the necessity for her to have that control. He explained that she was strengthened by the weakness she forced onto others and that they should also be careful because Lucy would not stop and she would always seek out more. She would come seeking others who were in association with me. He told them Lucy knew that I was alive and that it would only make her angrier now that help was being sought. The family was in silence as they looked at each other. The picture was becoming clearer because there wasn't any true mother that would inflict such pain and suffering on their own child. After all, Anna was caught up in the same web of deceit and possession as me. Anna was under her total control and being closer to her made it more difficult for Anna to be released from her grasp. However, the family's concern at this time was not Anna, it was me. They were concerned with getting me better and nothing else mattered. Mudeen gave the family verses to recite from the Quran, the holy book of Islam. He led them to believe that with the recital of the verses, they should begin to see a welcomed change within me. He told them I was spiritually strong and was staying alive due to the fight I had in me.

Mudeen had left the family with more questions than answers. I was still lying in bed and now, he had raised the validity of Lucy's objective. He had placed a stain on them that enveloped them. My family had spent so much money to get Mudeen here and there were still no signs of recovery.

In the days that followed, my mom and the rest repeatedly recited the verses over me, hoping to see a change, hoping that I would emerge from the depths from which I was being forcefully kept. They knew of the spirit called Kali Ma and they knew the power they were up against. They, being mere humans, were caught up in a battle that favored the otherworldly evil that the experienced Lucy was all too aware of. Lucy had total control. She had summoned the great Kali Ma into our midst and sought to destroy the sacred relationship that existed within a man, wife, and his family. She was the divider, the conqueror of the evil deeds that she had brought forth. Days wore on and, still, there were no signs of emergence from the hold on me. They burned the incense that was given by the priest from Brooklyn and wiped my body with the lavender with the hope that something would work.

My family had now tried three different religious factions, none of which had freed me from the grasp of an evil hold. They were beginning to wonder if this was it. My mother would not accept that, she would not come to terms of defeat and continued to recite verses from the Bible, the Quran, and the Bhagavad Gita, a sacred text in Hinduism. She had become obsessed with the notion of prayer. She tried everything she had within her disposal and yet, I continued to sleep. Each individual religion had taken a shot at reversing the evil that Lucy had cast but it was of no avail. Mom, preoccupied in her prayer, asked Ray, Stephen, and Marvin to ask their friends if they knew of anyone that would be able to help. They reached out to all they had known and no one was educated or experienced in the support that was specifically needed. Drew and Nancy grew tired and scared. They were afraid of losing me, their brother, especially from something in which they thought they had control over. They knew Lucy had invoked a vile and malicious threat to their beloved brother.

Stephen visited a Kali temple, with the hope of having the same evil be returned to where it had come and to better understand the strength and capabilities of Kali Ma. What he saw there was despicable, as he explained. He witnessed Kali Ma being invoked by her worshippers. He noticed that the followers of her evil would offer alcohol and cigarettes to the painted murti, a stone-carved manifestation of Kali Ma that was placed on a lofty mantle. She was an idol that was being prayed to, being revered, and exalted by her flock of faithful followers. He knew he could not have benefited from such a visit and he ran out of the temple as fast as he could. He was made aware that an evil, such as Lucy, had existed more commonly than what everyone had believed. There were thousands of followers that used the Goddess for personal gain and the destruction of others. His own religious beliefs were brought into question as he observed the followers accomplishing a feat of voluntary possession. Kali Ma was being summoned into the midst of their anticipated congregation. She was being gifted by the sacrifices of animals, that of human flesh, and that of liquor, and Stephen knew that he needed to forget what he had seen and sent a message to mom and the others to be aware. He knew they were up against evil, an evil that existed in Lucy. Lucy was not a typical summoner or conjurer; she could have possibly been Kali Ma herself. Her crude deeds were proof of that.

Stephen learned that Kali Ma wasn't a mere idol of worship, but she was a manifestation of the conjurer's needs. Stephen had witnessed in the temple various versions of the representation of Kali Ma. The name was just a name that was given to reflect the idea of those representations. Kali Ma's followers, in that specific temple, were filled with envy, jealousy, and hatred for others. They sought the help from the greatest manifestation known to them, one of Kali Ma.

It had been days since Mudeen had left and there were no changes to be found in me. My family maintained communication with Mudeen and he iterated that even though he was oceans apart, he was still working on helping me. He dedicated his time in prayer, in a battle for my life. They knew he had known more than what he had told them but also knew that his beliefs and religion did not permit him from freely divulging information of the otherworldly. He had told them that his gifts were derived from prayers, a lot of prayers. He had gained that status through communication through prayer and there were rules to be followed. The gifts he possessed were attained and could have easily been revoked if he had not maintained them for doing acts of good. There was an ethics code that those of high religious status needed to adhere to and Mudeen chose to abide by the laws given to him after receiving his religious fortitude. He knew what was needed to be done and accomplished the necessary feats without breaking his religious code of ethics.

Chapter Twelve

Around three o'clock one Saturday afternoon, mom and Drew were in the kitchen and Nancy sat on the chair in the living room while Stephen lay on the sofa bed beside me when I suddenly turned and sat up on the bed. Stephen immediately sprung off the bed and settled next to Nancy, who had just emerged from a drifted nap. She was shaken awake by the vibrations of Stephen's unanticipated wake-up call. They both looked at me with fear. They were afraid that I would somehow harm them. I looked at them with a questioned look as to suggest, "What are you all doing?"

They continued to look on in fear and I was confused in attempting to understand the looks on their faces. They then shouted for my mom and Drew who immediately came running through the floral curtains that divided the rooms. Nancy was still seated, Stephen sat next to her chair on the floor, and Stella and Drew stood next to them. They all were looking at me and I at them. No one spoke. The room remained silent and I could see the fear in their faces. My mom was still holding the large wooden spoon she had brought with her from the kitchen and I could see its trembling, as it reflected the emotions stirring within her body.

Marvin and Ray weren't there at the time. I assumed they had gone out to work. As the rest continued to peer their eyes onto me, I spoke. I said, "Hi, what are you all doing?" then smiled. They were still in amazement; they did not know what to think or what to believe. I said, "I'm hungry guys." The spoon dropped from the shaky hands that had held them and my mom came running over to the sofa bed. She gave me an embrace that I will remember all the days of my life. It was emotional, it was tight, it was as though she had poured all of her love for me into that embrace and it flowed through her arms as they were placed around me. She rested her head on my shoulder and she cried, she cried of love and of care. Being a mother, she knew I had returned. It was me, her son, not any spirit, not any possession, not anyone strange to her, just her son. With the tears flowing to her shirt, she turned to the rest of them and said, "It's David."

The skepticism on their faces told me everything I needed to know. I could have seen the look on Drew's face. She believed that I was not me, her expressed face denied herself the belief that it was. She, followed by Stephen and Nancy, slowly approached where I was anyway. They all asked if I was okay, how I was feeling, what I remembered, and if I knew how long I was sleeping for. I told them I had not remembered much except for bits and pieces, here and there. They said that it did not matter anymore and just then, my mom held my arm and led me to the kitchen. I was weak, I stumbled and wobbled to the kitchen where I sat on a chair at the dinette table as she asked me what I wanted to eat. She had just finished cooking something, so she placed a little on a plate and placed in front of me. I remember being hungry but I do not remember what I ate. What I do remember, was that I began crying at the kitchen table and that I asked my mother, "How are Anna and the kids?" She told me that she did not know and that they were focused on making sure I was okay. The rest of my family at home narrated to me what had taken place in the last few days and decided that we weren't going to speak about it again. After eating, I went to the bathroom, though feeling weak, and vomited everything I had eaten. Nancy and my mom thought it was normal as I had not eaten in days and my stomach rejected the food. I agreed with them and I continued to the shower and got dressed.

I remember very little of the time from when I initially got to Nancy's until after I woke up. There were fragments of seeing a bearded man and that of everyone reciting prayers over me but I could not piece together a complete understanding of that time.

My thoughts were of Anna and the kids and I needed to find out if they were okay. I called Anna's cellphone but would not get an answer. The phone would go directly to voicemail. I was heading out the door when mom asked me not to go, not now. She asked me to stay at home with them and get some rest and that I would go the next day. I told her, "You had said I was under some stupid possession for days now so why should I wait? A lot of time passed and I need to see my family." She did not agree with me, nor did Stephen and the others. They remembered the last time I was there did not end well. They made attempts to convince me not to go but I was stubborn and adamant on going. There was a renewed determination and fight in me. Although they had explained everything about Lucy, I was not discouraged. I had seen her evil capabilities. I had seen the power she had possessed but I was not afraid. I had lived in the same house with the devil of a woman and I knew she would not let Anna and the kids go. Drew and the others finally caved. They saw I had an improved grit within me. I "appeared wiser," as my mother put it. Although in a dreaming state, it appeared as though I had learned something from it. I knew what needed to be done so I bolted through the door and was on my way.

On my way there, there was a confused excitement that had filled inside me. I was anxious, excited, and overwrought, all while being apprehensive. There was renewed hope and confidence with the anticipation of reuniting with my family. Maybe I was naïve and had hoped that everything would be as it was before.

I arrived at what had been my home, the house where I had such great plans and dreams for a great future with Anna and the kids. I parked at the front and stared at the house. There was no activity, nothing stirred and it appeared abandoned. I was confused and looked on in dismay. I got out of the car and proceeded toward the front step while remembering the last moments I was there. In my mind, I could have pictured Lucy leaning against the guard rail of the stairs, I could have seen the officer questioning me, I could have seen Richard and Daniel taking a beating. The memory of when I was last there, a few days ago, did not deter me. I was stronger now, I felt invincible and continued to the front door. I placed the key into the locked door and slowly turned the handle. My heart was pounding as I geared up for another confrontation. As the door opened, I could see the inside of our living room. My eyes opened widely in disbelief as there was nothing there. I then opened the door all the way through and looked on in total shock. The house was empty. I could have seen the carpeted floors and the stains left from where the furniture had been. There were remnants of pieces of paper throughout the floor and scattered bits of accumulated dust in a few areas. The windows were bare, curtains gone, holes left from where the blinds were being held, and holes on the walls where picture frames had once made their home. The quiet house of no action, which was once filled with the vibrancy of life, had been transformed into a painted structure of uselessness.

As I made my slow but deliberate walk through my abandoned house, I kept thinking about what could have happened. I went into the kitchen that was once filled with the banging of pots and spoons and full of life and energy. It was now empty; the drawers and cabinets were bare and every last spoon, cup, and plate were gone. I proceeded upstairs to Kevin and Linda's rooms and again, there was nothing there. The crib, which had once housed my beautiful baby girl, had vanished. I could see the clean spots on the carpet where the legs of the crib had once stood. The rooms were vacant and abandoned. I proceeded to mine and Anna's bedroom and, again, there was nothing there. There were two pieces of torn clothing on the ground that represented the storm that had passed through the house. I returned downstairs and sat on the floor with my back leaned up against the wall in the dining room, where the buffet had once made its appearance known. The house was bare, desolate, and eerie. There were no pictures on the walls, no furniture, not anything in sight. My clothes were all gone, my personal belongings were taken, and I felt stripped. I was stripped of everything I had owned, that *we* had owned. Sitting on the floor and panning through the vacant rooms within the house, it occurred to me that I should call the bank to find out if I had any money left. To no surprise of mine, the bank account was closed and no longer existed. Every penny was withdrawn and the account I had ceased to exist. I had lost my family, my personal belongings, and my money. Everything was all gone.

I called Nancy and the others and, while the phone was on speaker, I was able to let them know what I had returned home to. They told me to not worry and to return to Nancy's, where they'd be able to discuss and help in any way that they could. I forced myself up from the floor and was making my way to the front door when I remembered the basement. I had forgotten, or it did not occur to me, to check the basement. I turned around and made my way toward the door. As I approached the door, I observed that it was open and quickly realized there was no one there. I contemplated a bit on entering and then thought out loud, "What the heck." I pulled the door open and started my way down the stairs. It had just been a few treads down when I noticed that it was also emptied. There was nothing there, same as the first and second floors.

As I continued to walk to the rear, where there were two bedrooms divided by a small linen closet, I noticed the doors were shut and a red handle from a broom was being used to prop the door closed. I removed the handle and pulled the door open. There was a rotten and foul odor that smelled like a latrine from the old days, an outhouse. I covered my nose and mouth with the inner part of my right arm, stifled my nose, and slowly walked in. Just barely looking, I observed a small red and dirty bowl lying upside down next to a crumpled piece of plastic on the floor. As I made my way towards the bowl, still covering my nose from the overwhelming stench, I kicked it over and to my disbelief, there was a pile of human feces. It was not of an adult but those of a child. I could not have believed my eyes. I stood there, wondering what or whose they could have been. I reached over to the light switch and quickly turned it on. I would then see a length of yellow and half-rusted chain coiled up in the corner of the room, being held firmly to the wall by a bolted silver hook. I was appalled and shocked by the sight that had shaken everything I had believed in. Within a second of seeing the chain, the bowl and, the plastic on the floor with the covered feces, my brain immediately understood and knew what it was. I knew they were that of Kevin's. I knew that the monsters had kept him in here. I knew that they had tied him up. I knew that they had beaten him. I knew that they had made him sit in his own feces and fed him in a bowl. He was treated like an animal. I knew because Kevin would have cried to be with me. I knew because he would have wanted to climb the stairs to where he knew he belonged. They kept him there to punish me and to threaten me. They had left the evidence behind because they knew I'd find it. They were leaving a message for me, that if I tried to find them, they'd hurt him even more. I walked out of the room and ran up the stairs to the first floor. I immediately took a deep breath as I had held it for so long in the basement. I was still in disbelief. I cannot, till this day, move past what I had seen in the basement.

The memories of the minute I was in there sit with me till today and have altered my life in more ways than I choose to ponder. Kevin had endured what no child, no human, should ever have to. The evil and despicable acts that were delivered upon him from another human would alter the way he would grow into becoming the person he was meant to be. The presence of his pain and suffering was felt through the walls of the room and transcended upon me with its fiercest blow, and I felt every inch of it. Whoever did this had meant for it to be this way, had meant for me to endure the pain, possibly to break me, to weaken me, to defeat me.

Chapter Thirteen

I walked inside the living room, sat on the floor, and leaned myself against the bare and dusty window sill. I was once again defeated by Lucy and I knew that she knew I was defeated. I could hear her voice again telling me, "I told you there was nothing you could do." Her evil voice kept ringing in my head and her presence was felt within the walls of the house. She was everywhere. She'd whisper in my ear constantly, "I told you there was nothing you could do." She had tormented me and she was victorious. I had become completely broken beyond repair and I allowed the voices to claim their hard-worked victory.

I couldn't bear the torture of her deadly whispers so I ran out to the back of the house. I again began to vomit the acidic taste of bile. The emptiness in my system had come to the surface and attempted to force its way out of my mouth. As I leaned over, hands on my knees, the bile was ingested back into my stomach from the sight of the plain, dirt-filled ground, where the barbeque grill once was. I saw the edges of burnt pictures, pictures of my once happy family that existed here. There were scraps of paper, clothing, burnt photos, and my personal hygienic supplies that resided once on the bathroom console. I knew then what happened to all my personal belongings. They were ritualistically burnt, or burnt out of spite and hatred that Lucy had for me. As of that moment, I did not know what I had done to make Lucy turn her wicked and treacherous ways unto me. She had devoted time, energy, and prosperous evil to satisfy her wickedly insane feelings she had for me. I questioned my personality. I questioned who I was and what I had done. What possibly did I do, or didn't do, to turn my wife's mother against me? I had always treated her daughter and her entire family with great respect. I went out of my way to ensure that they were all happy. I provided them a place to stay in my own home, although the basement, it was in my home. I pondered the years back, sifting through memories, attempting to identify a time in which I may have wronged her. I couldn't.

I sorted through the bits and pieces left of mementos of my family and held on to them as my treasures. I had chosen to return home with the intention of finding my family here again. Instead, I had found a house; a house with a roof, a floor, and a yard, but most definitely, not a home. An abandoned and discarded cube, that had once housed the love, the connection, the life, and the blossoming of a young and vibrant association, now stood there as a pillar of hatred and an omen of bad things that were coming.

I remained at the back of the house for a while and gathered as many pieces of the burnt items as I could, then returned inside. I walked through the first and second floor once more, savoring the moments as I did. It seemed that this might have been the last time I was going to walk these halls. It took me a while to do so, then I left.

I returned to my mom's and filled them in on what I witnessed at the house. They told me they were there to support me and that everything was going to be okay. I knew they were just trying to make me feel better and could not have known how I felt after seeing what I had seen. From my perspective, my life as I knew it was over because there was nothing left of me. I showed to them the remainders of the pieces of who I was. I showed them the mostly burnt photos and the scraps of pieces of myself that I had taken with me. After seeing what I had brought back, my mom and Nancy began their spiels of life. They started to narrate from the book of family life, the book that exists within every family when one is in need. They were telling me that life is tough and I needed to get the strength to move on and needed to forget and put everything behind me.

The information given had seemed so redundantly monotonous and did nothing to get me over the hurdle that sat still in front of me. How could I just forget about the life I built and the family I had been blessed with? Kevin, Linda, and Anna were my everything. They were my life support and, without them, I would cease to exist. The materialistic trinkets that were accumulated over time were just that, trinkets. It was my family that had really mattered. My life was about the four of us: Kevin, Linda, Anna, and I. The effervescence of the relationships we shared was as bright, prosperous, and hopeful as the future we were aiming to carve.

I excused myself from within the harmonious well-wishers, proceeded outside, and sat on a bench that had seemingly been placed for my anticipated arrival. I indulged myself in thoughts of what once was and what they could have possibly been. I made attempts to envision a future without Anna and the kids and I just couldn't. All roads and dreams led back to paving a path that would include us all. I sat there for the remainder of that gloomy afternoon sulking in my sorrows and all that had fallen into my lap.

I returned inside later that night and lay on the sofa bed which had become my comfortable resting nest. As I laid there, forcing myself to sleep, the whispering voices had returned. They had returned to torment me, to mock me, to kick me when I was down. I was already weakened from the events of the past day and the voices got the better of me. They got under my skin and I was scared. I was scared that they had returned now because I was already defeated. I did not have the strength to fight back and they had returned to finish the job. I was giving in. I had accepted that they won and Lucy was triumphant. As I surrendered to the unison whispers of darkness, I saw the pair of familiar eyes in the corner of the wall and ceiling. The compassionate pair that had been my guide and companion through my grief and sorrow had returned to share my demise. The pair looked at me with the same compassion as before, they felt my pain, my agony, and my surrender. They then started to weep. There were tears once again flowing freely along the walls. The walls were weeping. As the walls wept, I had remembered from their previous appearance that they were there more of a warning to me rather than a hazard.

As I have come to understand, the eyes from which the tears had flowed were a representation of myself and the tears were a manifestation of my feelings, of my strength, and of my resilience. The whispering and eerie voices represented all that was cruel and malicious. The voices represented the culmination of all the evils Lucy had released onto me. I remembered and then understood that the voices were defeated the first time I had seen those eyes and the weeping walls. The following times they were convincing me, they were urging me to continue and not give up. They had caused the eerie voices to retreat and they were fighting a seemingly winless battle. The receding of the tears represented my defeat and the retreat of the voices had signaled my victory. More often than not, there was a calm surrender from within me that allowed the voices their celebrated victory but I knew that it would be temporary. I knew, or I chose to believe, that I would eventually become victorious so I gave them their moment in the spotlight.

The weeping walls now appeared again and I thought to myself, "What could this now mean? Could this mean that I will once again have to face an unforeseen danger that lurked, or, was it a signal of my victory of recovery from a near-death experience?"

I wasn't afraid anymore. As walls continued to weep, I would stare into the glitter and melodious flow and slowly regain my sense of confidence and ambition. I would slowly begin to believe again that I was stronger than this, I was meant for more than this. The voices slowly vanished as the tears freely flowed. The manifestation of myself had been victorious and the weeping walls streamed with contentment. As I lay there, with the voices now gone, I was able to interpret the messages from these weeping walls. No words were spoken aloud, but the message was clear as day. They were telling me to fight for my family, they were telling me to get my ass off the bed and to not let the once dominant whispers of Lucy get to the better of me. The tears that flowed told me I had nothing more to lose and I should do my best to release Anna and the kids from the powerful hold that Lucy had on them. These weeping walls, my companion, my inner strength, had prevailed over my self-infliction of desolation and desperation. Through the thoughts of confidence and invincibility that the tears had given me, I was able to fall asleep with a renewed sense of hope.

Lucy had started a war and even though she may have won all the battles up until now, I had regained the fight in me through the understanding of the weeping walls. I had a renewed focus, a renewed sense of self-confidence and motivation, to have Lucy punished for destroying my family.

Chapter Fourteen

On that night, I slept better than any time I had slept in the past month. I awoke that morning and went into the kitchen where my mom, Drew, and Nancy were already awake. I sat down at the breakfast table with them and we discussed a plan to get my family back. We contacted Mudeen, who was back in Trinidad, and we told our plan to him. The plan was to rescue my family from Lucy. We planned to have him pray for Anna and the kids as he had done for me, with the hope that he can release her from the grasp of Lucy's. Mudeen agreed to help but asked one very important question. He asked us if we had wanted the evil to return to the person from which it came. We asked him what he meant. He let us know that the processes and steps Lucy had taken could also be reversed. It could have been reversed and placed on Lucy. All the things she had done to me would be returned to her. Kali Ma, whom she had summoned, would return the vengeance that she sacked on me, back unto her. We didn't quite understand what he exactly meant but the decision was mine. At the time, with everything that had happened and not fully understanding what he meant, I agreed to it. I told Mudeen yes. I would do anything to help Anna and the kids and if that meant returning to Lucy what she had sacked unto me, it was an easy decision. Mudeen let us know that it would take some time and that we needed to have faith and pray.

I spent that day with my mom, Drew, Stephen, and Nancy and we talked quite a bit. We were discussing the possibilities of where Lucy had taken Anna and the kids, or what she had done with them. We formulated a plan to begin looking. When Ray and Marvin arrived at home from work, we relayed to them what we had thought about and they agreed to help. It was about three o' clock that afternoon when we began driving to the places that I knew of, where Anna and I had taken Lucy when she wanted to go somewhere. There weren't many places and we needed to start somewhere. We drove to a street in Queens where I remembered Lucy had visited with someone once. We parked out front where we stalked the house. We were there to monitor the comings and goings of anyone at the house, to see if it would lead us to or give us an inclination as to where they could have possibly gone.

We weren't there very long when, to our surprise, we saw Lucy pull up in a taxi. She got out and made her way to the front door. The taxi driver parked and waited so we knew that she wasn't going to be very long. My eyes stared at her with so much hatred and disgust, I wanted to get out of the car and strangle her. I wanted to inflict pain and suffering upon her, I wanted vengeance. My mom saw the look on my face and calmed me down. She knew that I was extremely angry and said if I did anything to Lucy, I would never find Anna and the kids. I swallowed the anger because I knew she was right. I continued to ogle Lucy as someone from inside the house opened the door and Lucy entered. We did not get a look at the person on the other end due to the angle in which we sat.

After ten minutes or so, she emerged through the doors from which she had entered. She was carrying a wooden mortar and pestle. We all looked at each other thinking how strange the sight was. Why would she have with her a mortar and pestle? She got back into the parked taxi and it drove off. We began to follow her with the hope of being led to where Anna and the kids were. As we pulled up behind the privately-owned gypsy cab, the driver sped off and the traffic light at the corner blinked into its untimely red. Ray was driving at the time and he went through the traffic light in pursuit of the taxi. We did not travel more than two blocks when we heard the sounds of police sirens at the rear. Ray pulled over to the side and we needed to abandon the chase. After receiving a summons from the unwelcomed officer, we returned to the house that we had stalked.

We all approached the front and I laid my finger on the doorbell. A lady opened the door and asked who we were. We gave her a short explanation and she let us in. She put us to sit in a little area in her home, apparently designated for short visits by temporary visitors. She joined us and we started to ask a series of questions. The first question asked was, "How do you know Lucy?" She replied that Lucy was her sister. After giving us this information, we were shocked. We did not know Lucy had a sister. This was news to us.

The lady, Sandy, began to cry while explaining to us that Lucy had done evil acts to her as well and that we should not mess with her. We told her we weren't there for Lucy, we just wanted to know where Anna and the kids were. She said although Lucy was her sister, she hated her. She had done unspeakable acts of evil against her and ruined her family. She lived alone and it was due to Lucy having done this to her. We weren't quite interested in what Sandy had to say because we had already developed an instant resentment for her since she was Lucy's sister. She said when Lucy wanted something, she'd take it using any means necessary. Sandy told us a little of what happened to her and her family and we listened. We listened to the lady cry. We heard of the time when Lucy had summoned other spirits to invoke unto her. We asked, "Why?" Sandy said that she had known Lucy for a very long time and she was a very jealous and envious person. She did not like to see people live happily. She told us about the various people Lucy would help in their hometown village in Guyana. Her help was not that of a typical nature but one that helped the wicked and cruel people of their village and neighboring ones. She would have done so for rewards, gifts, and most importantly, control. She wanted people to know how powerful she was and she was successful in garnering the respect for being a pundit of her trade. Her sister told us of the times she separated families, forced husbands to leave their wives, wives to leave their husbands, and villagers to lose possession of their land, all through her chants and summoning of evil. Her sister also told us that at certain times, she thought Lucy may have been the devil herself. She said the acts that she had witnessed were so despicable and sinful, it would make our skin crawl.

Lucy was a master of her sinister craft and she was out to get me. I had taken her most precious belonging and she wanted her back. Anna had fallen in love with me and Lucy was threatened by my existence. I had gotten too close to Anna and she had lost the control she had on her. Lucy knew she could not have controlled me because Anna was now disobeying her orders of wants and listening to mine. Anna had placed her on a back burner and she couldn't have that. She was going to stop at nothing to make me suffer, to make Anna return to her submissive ways, and to control Kevin and Linda into taking care of her every spiteful need.

We were beginning to understand a little more about Lucy and the type of person she was. We gave Sandy a bit more information about what had happened to me and she recommended that we speak to a woman by the name of Rachel. She said Rachel would be able to help us and would have a lot more information than she was able to provide. We asked Sandy why she was helping us and she simply replied, "I want Lucy to be stopped." She said everyone who had known Lucy was afraid of her. They had heard of the stories of her from Guyana and the various evils she placed on others to have her way. She warned us of the evils that Lucy had summoned in the past and that she was capable of a lot more than we thought as she had seen and witnessed the acts conducted by Lucy her entire miserable life. She gave us the address for Rachel and we left.

After leaving Sandy's house, I remember being relieved in small ways. I remember the feeling of accomplishment and the feeling of clarity; it was becoming clearer to me who Lucy actually was. We proceeded to the address given to us and we got there just about seven o'clock that night.

We observed the house where we arrived and saw that it was converted to a Hindu temple. There were representations made of painted and beautifully carved depictions of Lord Hanuman, Lord Shiva, and Goddess Lakshmi, placed next to a huge and picturesque white elephant. The revered and stone manifestations, or murtis, were representative of the symbolism of Hinduism and peace. They filled the yard with variations of orange, yellow, and white and depicted the innocence that was expected within the walls beyond. The depictions served as a clear sign of protection and allowed for a certain sense of tranquility. The front door was garlanded and there were beautiful multi-colored flowers that decorated the small rectangular landscaped front just beyond the fence. As we approached the temple of a house, a woman walked towards us, greeted us, and asked if she could be of help. We explained who we were and after a little hesitation, she invited us inside. As we entered through the front door, we were greeted by two little girls that were playing in a little area within the home. They were full of life, energy, and dynamism, and reminded me so much of Kevin and Linda. They held on to the woman's dress, gently tugging and saying, "Mommy, we, we, we're hungry." The woman called out to her husband, Tom, and he took the kids to the back. We sat together with the woman and she told us that she was Rachel. We told her again who had sent us and we were hoping that she could give us more information. Rachel jokingly asked, "How much time do you have?" We knew she meant that there was so much to tell that it was going to take a long, long time. We all had a small chuckle and I replied, "Please give us the shortened version." She humbly smiled and said, "Sure."

She started by saying that she was raised in a small village in the country of Guyana and that she was an energetic, young, and ambitious woman. She was a teenager in school and had loved a boy who had also loved her. She said back then families were old fashioned and a lot stricter and more protective, especially of the girl children. She told us about her love for this boy, Tom, and his love for her and how their relationship was not accepted by society. Tom was Muslim and she was Hindu. In those days, inter-religion relationships were not widely accepted, but two people of different religions had fallen in love. They struggled with the members of their own families. His family did not accept her and her family did not accept him. Rachel said everything began when she got pregnant. She knew the baby would have been rejected by the families and also by society, especially after knowing her relationship with the person whom she loved was also one of controversy.

Rachel and Tom decided to leave the village in pursuit of life elsewhere. They planned carefully and eloped on a Sunday afternoon whilst their families took afternoon naps. They loved each other and wanted to be together. They wanted to start a family and knew they couldn't in the village they were in. They had decided to go somewhere where no one knew who they were, where they'd be able to have the child and begin their new lives. Tom started a new job in farming and Rachel stayed at home taking care of herself and her unborn child. Rachel continued to tell us that they made very little friends because they mostly kept to themselves. She said she had gotten sick and there was no major hospital for her to visit and heard about a village doctor. They had heard that the doctor was famous and was a go-to person in the village. People went to the doctor because of the experience she possessed and because she had helped many people before.

One day, Tom took Rachel to the well-known doctor and this is where she met Lucy. There was no doctor's office or anything of the sort, it was her house – a rusted galvanized roof that covered a wooden box. It was an entire house that was no bigger than that of a studio apartment. There were no trees nor plants in the small fenced-in yard and the ground was made of a packed and smoothened clay. The one and only window at the front was boarded up and the darkness from within could have been seen from the spaces within the boards. The people from the village would come to her house when they sought advice or when they needed her help. She had also delivered babies before, for other people in the village. Rachel was very young, inexperienced, pregnant, sick, and needed help. As they entered the house toward the middle of the village, she was greeted by Lucy herself. Rachel said that Lucy took a special liking to her and immediately offered her help. Lucy meditated and waved her hands in the air while she chanted out the name Kali Ma continuously. Rachel said she appeared to be praying for her. Rachel, being unaware, sat there, listened, and participated in the requests being asked of her from Lucy.

After hours had passed, Rachel had felt better. Lucy had made her better and she began to have trust in her. Lucy offered her support and would come to Rachel's place to visit. She would constantly bring food, gifts, and medicine for Rachel and Tom. They developed a good relationship, and over time, as the baby was closer to being born, Lucy would stay over at Rachel's. She became her midwife.

Close to the end of the last trimester, Rachel grew very sick. She vomited constantly, she had diarrhea, nausea, and had no appetite. Lucy would tell her that it was normal, to not worry, she was there for her. She continued to give her food and gifts, and her chanting had become a daily routine. There were days that Rachel felt good and days that she felt horrible. One day, while Tom was at work, Rachel got very, very sick and Lucy took her to her place. She began chanting and Rachel was in and out of consciousness. Lucy told her it was time and that childbirth was imminent. She placed her on the bed and began her daily chants.

That was the last thing Rachel remembered before she was awakened by the loud cries of Lucy, who was sitting on a chair at the side of the bed. She would cry and shout, "No, no, no, no, no, no, no, no, no!" She would tap her hands on her knees and her feet to the floor and cry. Rachel looked up at her and asked to see her baby. Lucy looked back at her and said, "The baby was still-born." Rachel screamed out in pain. She was just given information that her baby had died during childbirth. She was in pain; she cried and screamed, again and again. She was hurt. Lucy sat there and disingenuously cried her eyes out, giving Rachel the perception that she cared deeply about what had happened. Rachel explained to us that she wished that she knew then, what she knew now. She would have been able to see right through Lucy. She stated that she was young, naïve, and unsuspecting.

As we sat there listening to Rachel, her memories of a past time came to the surface and tears of sorrow had filled her cheeks. Tears had begun to flow from the eyes of Nancy and my mother. We all felt her pain and we knew she was telling the truth. Her husband came into the room and placed his arms around her and said to not worry. He looked at her, wiped her tears away with his shirt, and he told her to continue. He left her with us and went about his way.

As she continued, she said she asked Lucy what had happened. Lucy told her that her body was weak and with her being sick, she had passed on an infection to the baby, who died even before birthing. Lucy told her to not worry about it and that she needed to get lots of rest because her body was still weak. Rachel had believed everything she said, there was no reason to believe otherwise.

The day had come and gone and life had settled into normalcy in the village. Rachel continued to recover and Tom continued to work. With much emotional struggle, they continued living in the village. After that horrible day when Lucy had told Rachel she had lost the baby, Lucy became isolated. The people of the village knew she was in the house but did not see her or hear from her. Her husband, Richard, did everything. He went to the grocery store and he took care of everything outside of the house while Lucy stayed indoors. Months upon months had passed and Lucy made very few appearances outside. When people of the village did see her, it was for just a moment. She sat on her partially hidden front porch that was blocked in by a galvanized and wooden railing that created a shield from any passersby.

Tom and Rachel had become distant with each other after the loss of the baby. Tom did everything he could to console and comfort

Rachel, but she became secluded. The absorption of loss had taken over her and she had become ill. She went crazy. She couldn't bear the loss of her baby and it took her mind. Everyone in the village referred to Rachel as the "crazy woman." Whispers of insanity paved the sidewalks when she walked and everyone stayed away.

A year had passed and, suddenly, Lucy announced to the village that she had a baby girl. No one was allowed to see the baby because she was ill and needed seclusion due to health issues. Word spread fast amongst the villagers and eventually caught the ears of Tom and Rachel. After hearing the news, Tom and Rachel rushed over to Lucy's house and asked to visit the baby. Lucy vehemently denied them and said she couldn't allow it. She said the baby was ill and couldn't have visitors due to the risk of infection. Tom and Rachel knew something was fishy but did not indulge themselves into an argument.

As months rolled on, Tom and Rachel eventually moved back to where they were originally from. They thought that after so much time had passed, everyone in their home village would have to accept their relationship for what it was. They were moving back whether the village accepted it or not.

About four years had passed and life had gotten back to a norm. Rachel had gotten over her sicknesses and she was not the "crazy woman" anymore. They started afresh and before long, Rachel was pregnant again. She and Tom had gotten over the loss of the baby, for the most part, and they were able to start over, albeit somewhere else.

Another two years came and went and Tom and Rachel decided to go to a fair that was in a close-by village, a much larger and more populated village than theirs. They got their little girl dressed and left early in the day so they could make the most of it. After arriving at the fair, they noticed there were hundreds and hundreds of people from all over who had come to the fair and appeared to be enjoying the various festivities. There were rollercoasters, bumper cars, and jungle gyms. The day was as beautiful as it could get; the sun was out, there was a gentle breeze, and the presence of life was felt as everyone participated in a series of games. Tom had won a beautiful stuffed penguin for his little one and Rachel was enjoying the quality time with the family. While walking through the crowds, they saw Lucy and Richard and also saw, to their surprise, a beautiful little girl walking with them, holding their hand. As they approached closer to where they were, Lucy caught the glance of Rachel and attempted to speedily dart through the crowd. She couldn't, there were too many people and she couldn't have gone far due to the thick gatherings. Tom and Rachel quickly caught up to them and the introductions had begun. Rachel introduced her daughter, "This is Rita," she said. Lucy and Richard looked at each other and was surprised that Tom and Rachel had another baby after all that had happened. Rita was pre-occupied as she was looking elsewhere at a clown that was performing close by. Her dark plaited hair was faced toward them and they were curious and anxious to see her face. Lucy then introduced her little girl, "This is Anna," and she turned around.

When Anna turned around, Rachel and Tom looked at each other in shock. There was a striking resemblance to Rachel. Anna had the same complexion, the same eyes, the same cheekbones, the same lips, and the same nose as Rachel. The resemblance was too much of a coincidence. Rachel and Tom immediately knew Anna was theirs. They knew she was their child that was stolen from them years ago by Lucy.

The room in which we were seated went silent for a second. My mom, Nancy, and I looked at each other and smiled, but then tears immediately began to flow. Rachel looked at us like we were crazy people. She stopped telling her story and asked us, "What happened? Why are you all in tears?" As we looked at her, my mom moved from next to me, sat next to her, and gave her an immense hug. Rachel was confused. We had realized that Anna was her daughter and simultaneously, we figured out what Lucy had wanted. We felt a sense of relief, in a little way. Rachel didn't know what was going on. Nancy broke the news to her. She simply said, "We know Anna, we know who Anna is." Rachel still looked on in confusion. We told her that I was Anna's husband and we were here because of Anna. We had come seeking out Lucy and instead, we found Anna's birth mother. Rachel began to cry after hearing the news about Anna. She had found her long-lost daughter, her daughter who had been believed to be gone forever. She yelled out to Tom in the kitchen and he came running. She broke the news and explained to him who we were. He himself started to shed tears as he also knew he had found his long-lost daughter. She paused for a moment, then began to ask questions about Anna. She was attempting to get to know her daughter. She wanted to know where she was, where she had been, how beautiful she was, and how intelligent she was. She wanted to know everything about Anna. Her anxiety and excitement showed and we answered as many questions as we could. We told her that we'd bring photos to show to her and we'd give her more information, but as of now, she needed to continue with her story.

Rachel continued with her story. Back at the fair, everything had immediately come into focus. Tom and Rachel knew that Lucy had taken Anna away from them. They knew Anna was their baby who was pronounced dead by Lucy years ago. Everything began to make sense to them. They immediately understood and knew that Lucy was evil and that she was responsible for her sickness, for her being called "crazy woman," and for the near-death experiences she sustained every other day. They immediately understood and were not naïve anymore. They knew the chanting by Lucy was that of devil worship. They knew everything. Lucy and Richard said they needed to get going and they did. Tom and Rachel were left standing there and knew there was nothing they could do to prove it. They dazedly pushed their stroller with Rita, navigating through the unsuspecting crowds of people. They returned to their little village knowing the truth but also knowing there was nothing they could do. Such things or things of such nature are common occurrences in third world countries and going to the authorities would be more detrimental. Tom and Rachel also knew that Lucy was revered and respected in her village and everyone had thought of Rachel as the "crazy woman." Years had already passed anyway and they had learned to live with it. Rachel ended by saying they saved money and moved to the United States after that. They now had three daughters – Rita, Melanie, and Susan and after many years had passed, their life had come to a settling ease and they were able to put their thoughts of Anna behind them.

Rachel invited all of us to stay for dinner that night with the hope that we could all exchange stories of Anna and Lucy. She wanted to find out more about Anna and we wanted to find out more about Lucy. The afternoon was a little uncomfortable for everyone. It was a bittersweet afternoon since it was now revealed what Lucy's true intentions were. On the sweet side, we knew Lucy's intentions were not to harm the kids but on the bitter side, she wanted them all for herself. She also wanted to have Anna under her control so that she could control the kids through her.

We didn't think of it before, but by observing Rachel, she reminded us a lot of Anna. The way in which she spoke, her nose, and her eyes were that of Anna's. We were sure that Rachel was Anna's mother.

During dinner, we spoke of what had transpired over the past few weeks and Rachel grew very upset. She wasn't going to allow Lucy to get away this time. She wasn't aware that Lucy also lived in New York because they had never crossed paths since the revealing night at the fair, many, many years ago. We explained to Rachel that Lucy's sister was the one who had revealed to us where to find her. She told us to not trust the sister because Lucy and she were from the same village and the sister would complete dirty deeds commanded by Lucy. We told Rachel to not worry due to the sister evidently turning against Lucy. We all chatted for a long while and then left.

On our way home, we had a renewed sense of accomplishment. We knew of Lucy's intentions and that provided a little comfort, knowing that they were close. The day was a successful one. We got home very late that night and departed to our personal spaces in the house. I laid on the sofa bed and forced myself to sleep. Through the anxiety I had felt from the course of the past day, I was looking forward to the morning.

I had, or *we* had, come to understand a lot more than we did before. We were aware of Lucy's intentions and we knew why she was doing all of this. All along, we thought she was out to get me and I was the object of her hatred, but we now knew that she was after the kids. I knew I had to get the kids away from her. I knew I had to get Anna away from her. She may have had evil on her side, but we had the strength of hope, faith, and our family connection. Lucy was planning the same thing that she had done with Anna and her parents. She had gotten older and wanted someone young to be able to take care of her in her latter stages. Her plan was to use Anna, Kevin, and Linda as her personal puppets to satisfy her evil, deadly, and selfish desires.

Morning came and we had our seemingly planned morning

gathering in the kitchen. Stephen, Drew, and my mom all went to work and Nancy and I sat alone discussing the events of the day before. As we sat at the kitchen table, Mudeen called and informed us that he had started the praying that would allow Anna to be released from the grasp of Lucy. We were glad to hear that and as we spoke, we informed him of the information we had gathered. He told us that he had known all that we had told him, with the exception of knowing who Anna's real mother had been.

Chapter Fifteen

The meetings in my mother's kitchen slowed and as each day passed, everyone slowly began to transition themselves back into their routine reality. Life had seemingly come to a crawl for me, minutes would last hours, hours would last days, days would seem like weeks, and weeks would seem like months. Mudeen would eventually stop calling and Anna and the kids were still nowhere to be found. I returned to Lucy's sister several times to ask her if she knew where Lucy was located, but she did not appear to know. We searched the streets of New York, starting from one end of a street to the other, looked in every driveway, and every nook and cranny, but there were no signs of them. I grew lonely and isolated myself with the thoughts of Anna and the kids. I dealt with a daily torture of truth that had separated me from them. There were days I visited the house in which we lived with the farfetched hope of possibly meeting Anna there, hoping that she would be revisiting the past, just as I was. The bank had placed a sticker on the window that I did not care to read. The house stood in its own space and appeared to have been singled out for the dwelling of the devil. It appeared to have been under a dark cloud that housed the dirtiest of deeds. The subtle wind that blew appeared to have avoided the house. The dry leaves would blow about on the street and the neighbor's yards, but there would be no movement as such from the house I lived in. There was a dark and cold feeling that emitted from the house caused by the evil that was done there.

I began working shortly after the night we last spoke with Mudeen and would continue to do so in the next few months to come. I would visit the address where we had seen Lucy when she visited her sister. I would spend hours there every afternoon, with the hope of seeing her so I could follow her. I remember making sure that the gas tank was totally filled up before I did, just in case she showed. I would have been able to follow her to any lengths she went to if the tank was full. I would return to my mom's every afternoon and cry my eyes out before falling asleep. She and the others did everything to comfort me. They never complained, they never faltered, and they even lost many hours, even days, of sleep on my behalf. This had become a nightly occurrence. Mudeen's praying did not appear to work. We had placed too much hope in him and he eventually stopped calling. Each morning, I woke up feeling more defeated than the last. I was completely broken and my level of motivation and inspiration were at their lowest.

It had been about three months and there were still no signs of Anna, the kids, or even Lucy. Day after day, my hope faded more and more. I wasn't crying or sulking much anymore. I began writing letters to Kevin, Linda, and Anna with the hope that one day they would be able to read and understand what I was feeling. I poured my heart out in words, penned in black, that fell on blank paper and deaf ears. I had missed them so much. Each day that passed would squeeze a little life out of me. My heart was becoming cold and my faith in the world was slowly being reduced. I had not done anything in my life to deserve the pain I had felt. Days and weeks went by and my longing for them increased. My silent prayers would fill my days to ensure the well-being of the three most precious people in the world.

Life, it seemed, had become normal again, except that Anna and the kids weren't in it. I started saving some money again as my days and nights were moving into a future of emptiness. I remember throwing up almost every day and my eyes were swollen all the time, the tears I had shed could have filled a river. I had begun to believe that Lucy had taken Anna and the kids to Guyana and I knew if she did, all hope would be lost. I slowly began to piece myself together. I remembered my love for Anna, I remembered what I had seen in the basement with what they did to Kevin, I remembered my little angel's face and slowly, I was beginning to put the pain aside. I reread the notes I had penned for Kevin and Linda and I crumpled and tossed each one of them. I spoke to myself, out loud, "You are stronger than this, you have to fight for what you believe in." Slowly, I was able to pull myself together and was again ready for anything. Lucy had defeated me for the umpteenth time and I had conceded. The law was not an option as I had a record and no one believed me. They would not have seen through my eyes what I had seen. They wouldn't have understood nor believed that I was where I am because of an elderly woman. They wouldn't have trusted in the existence of an otherworldly force that laid in wait for my destruction. My belief and faith had all but vanished, but now, the old David was returning. I had begun to see things clearer.

Each day passed and my thoughts were filled with nothing but my family. I missed them so much. I missed Kevin, Linda, and Anna, and I prayed for them to be found. It had been six months and life came to an unsettling ease. I bowed my head, knelt to the ground, put my palms together, and prayed, *"God, please return my family from the evil of Lucy. God please, I will give anything, I will do anything. I promise I will never ask from you anything, ever again. I will forever be in your debt and I will continue to be good. I will help people, I will ensure that Anna, Kevin, and Linda never suffer. Please God, please God, I beg of you, please return them to me."*

I could not sit there and do nothing. I made attempts to engage in the unremarkable ideas that passed my time. I drove through street after street, avenue after avenue, day after day, and yet, I discovered nothing. I had begun to abandon the faith and trust I had maintained in God. I spoke out loud to Him. I argued with Him. I cursed at Him for neglecting me in my greatest time of need. I argued with Him for abandoning Anna, Kevin, and Linda. From my perspective, it did not appear that He was the most powerful or the most supreme. He was allowing an evil within an evil to overwhelm my family and my faith in Him was being diminished.

I was sitting at home one afternoon on the bench at the back of my mom's house and remembered an old friend, Susan, where I had worked. I remembered that she was heavily involved with the church and decided to reach out to her. I contacted Susan and made the time to see her. I went to her house and explained everything that had happened and she said she'd speak to the heads of the church and ask them if there was anything they could do. I thanked her for listening to me and pleaded with her to help me.

It hadn't been more than two days when Susan called me. She said she had spoken to the members of the church and they were gathering their high councils to set a date where I'd need to go to church and join them in their prayer in an attempt to rid Lucy of her control. We set a date and time for that Wednesday and I went to the church.

I met with Susan in the parking lot and she held me by the wrist and escorted me through the massive and beautiful doorways of the church. As we entered, I could see the gathering of approximately a dozen men and women. They were all dressed in white long robes and wore beads around their necks. As we approached them, they gathered, formed a large circle, held each other's hands, and asked me to join them. I did as they asked and they started reciting verses from the Bible. As they prayed, I prayed. I prayed for the return of my family, I prayed for the release of Lucy's grasp. They prayed and recited the verses of the Bible with passion. They were loud and they were in unison.

I remember looking at them and thinking, "They are doing this for me. They set aside their daily routine and planned an event of prayer for which I was the beneficiary." They continued for about an hour or so and then let go of each other's hands and put me to sit on a very long, wooden, and glossy bench. Susan sat beside me as the man in white spoke to me. He said that I needed to continue with my praying and that God would never let me face this battle alone. He was my protector and savior and I needed to believe in him. I needed to believe that God would never abandon His child, especially when He was needed the most. I believe him. I knew I needed to pray harder and more often and I also knew that God had not deserted me. I thanked Susan and the men in white for their gathering and their help and was on my way. I returned to my mom's that afternoon and secluded myself from everyone, crawled onto the sofa bed, and laid my head to rest.

About a week had passed and I was at work one day while driving when my phone rang. I looked at the number and it was not one that was stored in my contacts – a strange but local number. I answered the phone and there was someone on the other end but they were not talking, they listened. I kept saying, "Hello," but still, no one would answer. The phone then hung up and I continued on with my day. A few days later, again at work, the phone rang and again, I picked up. There was someone on the other end but still would not speak.

In my thoughts, I knew it was Anna. I knew she was on the other end and she wasn't speaking. I asked, "Anna, is that you?" There was still no reply. About a minute had passed with no reply and then the phone hung up. I knew it was Anna, every fiber of my being knew it was her. I also knew she would call again. A small glimmer of hope had now entered me. I had begun to believe again. I remember telling myself, "David, a little while ago, you were about to forsake God and everything that He stood for, and now, He is the one that is making you believe again."

"It's amazing," I thought to myself. It's amazing that being a mere human allows us to choose sides based on strength and the probability of victory. We subconsciously ignore the trivial beings and place emphasis on the powerful and the triumphant. I was about to abandon the faith and trust I had in God when things weren't going my way and started to believe in Him again due to a glimpse of His mercy and understanding, simply through a phone call received. When things don't go the way I expect them to, this is the time I should have the strongest of beliefs, the most powerful faith should overwhelm me, because that is the time when God is closest to me and will never neglect me.

The possibility of a reunion with my family had now become much more hopeful. My faith was being strengthened once more and I placed my trust in God that He knew what He had planned.

I didn't mention anything to my mom and the others because they knew, or they thought they knew, I was doing better and moving on with my life. About a week had passed and I was at the grocery store when my phone rang. I answered and there was silence from the other end. I decided to break the ice with the anonymous caller. I said, "Hello, Anna? Is that you? Please talk to me, I know it's you." The caller finally spoke and replied with a very coarse but low-toned voice, "Hello, It's Anna." The sound of her voice sent a spark of electricity through my entire body. My eyes immediately filled with tears from the happiness and relief I felt. I had never been happier to hear the sweet sound of Anna's voice. An angel had spoken and my heart had received a shot of rejuvenation that I desperately needed. I told her that she could call me anytime, whenever she wanted, whatever time, night or day. She said, "Okay," and then quickly hung up. I had become so excited. After so much time, there was actually some hope left.

In the coming days, Anna began to call more frequently. We were able to have conversations, not for very long, but full sentences were spoken. The feeling I got felt like we had started dating all over again. The conversations we had were comparable to that of the conversations we had when Anna and I had first met. I wanted to ask so badly about the kids but I refrained myself from doing so. The refrain was probably one of the most difficult things I've ever done in my entire life. I needed to know how the kids were, but I also did not want to scare Anna away or get her angry with me in any way. Each time we spoke, after the phone call, I'd shed tears of happiness.

One Sunday afternoon, Anna called and we were able to talk for a while. She appeared to be the old Anna. We talked, laughed, and reminisced. I remember thinking to myself that I had her where I wanted her. The momentum had built up for me to ask about Kevin and Linda. My nerves were tense, my heart skipped beats at a time, but I finally broke the question, "How's Kevin and Linda doing?" Anna answered promptly and to the point, "They're okay, they're good," she replied. I was relieved and asked when could I see them. Anna started telling me that she had been calling me unbeknownst to Lucy. She began to tell me that since they were taken away, Lucy had treated her badly and kept her as her personal gofer. She told me Lucy had a hold on her. At times she'd be able to think on her own and other times it would appear that she needed to follow every command of Lucy's. Whenever she would appear to be unresponsive, or argumentative, it wouldn't last long. In some way, Lucy would observe and reel her back in. She told me at one time, Lucy had taken her to a Kali temple where she was forced to participate in a ritual that involved the sacrifice of a chicken. Anna said it was probably the most difficult thing she had ever had to participate in. She said she wanted out of the grasp of Lucy. Anna had realized that Lucy was evil, the instigator of everything, the doer of misdeeds against her family, against me, and against the kids. She had forced an unimaginable evil unto us that caused a great divide. Anna became furious and said she wanted out. She made sure to tell me she needed to act normal and subside in the presence of Lucy so that she couldn't figure out that she was not totally under her control anymore. Anna ranted for a while and said that she was happy I was okay and that we needed to get the kids away from Lucy. I was happy to hear those words from Anna because I received the assurance I needed. Anna was just as much a victim of Lucy's wicked intentions as I was. She had been going through similar difficulties as I had been, possibly worse.

Anna understood the importance of keeping Lucy at bay, keeping Lucy in the dark with the revelation of my involvement. Anna told me that she understood why Lucy was doing what she was doing. She told me that Lucy hated me, she despised me because I was smarter and I had provided Anna with more than she ever could have. I gave her children and I provided a house that we made into a home. I had been proud and Anna had succumbed to my ways and abandoned Lucy's. Anna said that Lucy began to acknowledge that she was becoming older and if she had lost Anna to me, she would not have anyone to care for her in her old age. She wanted to use Kevin and Linda just as she had done with Anna years ago. Unlike others, Lucy was armed with weapons far beyond our knowledge and understanding. She had the advantage of evil and sinister capabilities. Her evil was not supernatural but was representations of the evils that could be given life through the disturbance of peace through hatred and anger. The baleful deeds that she performed took a hold of her and embedded itself into her, became a part of her, grew into her, and was strengthened by her belief and prayer to an otherworldly manifestation known as Kali Maa. Her heart had become as dark as her complexion and her soul was overridden with and consumed by the devil she had created from within herself. A once normal human being had allowed herself to be consumed by pride, envy, and jealousy.

Anna and I made plans to meet, along with Kevin and Linda, the following Sunday at a park on the corner of Sutphin Boulevard and the Van Wyck Expressway. We set a time but she was clear, she made sure to tell me, if she didn't show up, it would not be because of her, it would be because she needed to ensure Lucy did not have any inclination of what she was up to. We both knew and understood if Lucy had found out that she was even talking to me, she would have done something to drive a wedge further into our attempted reunion. It would have spelled the end of us, probably for good this time. We both agreed and the plan was set for Sunday.

During that week, I remember how uneasy I was. I was anxious, excited, impatient, and scared. The days of the week seemed to have dragged along. I hadn't seen Kevin, Linda, or Anna in over six months and the time had finally arrived where I had the opportunity to see them. As the day drew closer, I became very scared. I was afraid that Lucy would find out and the entire dream would be over. During the week, I prayed often, I prayed hard, I prayed for everything to work out with my family. I finally filled in my mom and the others of what was taking place and they got very worried for me. They knew all that they had endured before and wasn't looking forward to repeating the same scenario. They warned me, they pleaded with me. They told me to give it time and wait to see how things played out. I told them I had been talking to Anna for about two weeks and I knew what I was doing. They were still very worried. They reminded me of when I was debilitated, in bed, under Lucy's control, and possessed. I told them I was stronger now and had no intentions of going through that again.

Nancy appeared to be a bit more bothered than anyone else and decided to call Mudeen. After filling him in on everything, he decided that he wanted to meet with us. We were fortunate that Mudeen was in New York at the time, attending a seminar. We arranged for him to come over on Saturday, the day before I was supposed to meet with Anna and the kids. I was glad that he was coming over as I had not had a chance to thank him for what he had done for me earlier. I felt as though he was the one responsible for my healthy recovery. Nancy and the others most definitely believed that as well.

Saturday rolled around and Mudeen came to the house. He entered through the doorways, greeted us, "Assalamu-Alaikum," walked over to me, and put his arms around me. He said two things to me, two things that define who I am today, something that I remember in times of despair. First, he said, "You are one of the strongest people I know," and secondly, "Family is the strongest bond in the world."

I was happy to hear that. Those words, in many ways, empowered me. They gave me strength, they boosted my enthusiasm, my ability to accomplish, and my ability to have hope. Mudeen was genuinely happy to see me. He had never seen me this way. He knew of me in bed, he knew of me as the person whom he had helped, he knew me as the possessed and bedridden one. The guileless look exhibited on his face told me everything I needed to know. After a lengthy embrace, we sat down and everyone gathered in a meeting of the minds. Mudeen was already up to speed on everything and he knew he needed to give me protection, spiritual protection, from Lucy.

Mudeen asked if there was anything that I had, something which I wore or which I kept with me for twenty-four hours a day. I thought about it for a while and could not come up with anything. He then looked at my right wrist and observed that I was wearing a silver bracelet. He asked if I had worn that all the time. I replied "No." He said that I should. He slid the bracelet off my hand, placed it between both his hands, closed his eyes, and began to recite words of the Quran. He meditated and rotated the bracelet while chanting words of the Lord. This lasted for a few minutes and when he was done, he gave the bracelet back to me and told me I should never take it off. He said he had placed protection of a special kind that would be able to ward off evil and help me with the protection from Lucy. I agreed to never take it off as Mudeen said his goodbyes and was on his way. We spent the rest of that Saturday afternoon talking about the scheduled rendezvous with Anna.

Later that night when everyone retreated to their bedrooms, I lay on the sofa bed and highly anticipated the rise of the morning sun. I don't think I slept because I was too anxious. As the time drew closer to our meeting time, I shaved, showered, and left the house about an hour in advance. It would have taken about ten minutes to get to the park where Anna had said we'd meet but I wanted to get there early. Shortly after I arrived at the park, I sat on a bench awaiting their much-anticipated arrival. Anna had said that she'd be there around noon and I got there at a quarter after eleven. I was thinking of things to say to them. I wondered if they had forgotten me, I wondered if they would even recognize me. I grew impatient and thoughts of Anna and the kids filled my mind. I remembered the precious times we had spent with each other and was hopeful they could return. The park was filled with kids and their families. It was an overcast day but signs of life and enthusiasm had filled my being with sunshine and warmth. The time had finally come to the reunion with my children, who had been lost for over six months.

The time that had passed from the moment I was sent to jail to now, will forever haunt my memory but I sometimes use it as a tool, a weapon, to remind myself where I had been and what I needed to endure. I use it as an inspiration to fulfill greater objectives and to guide me through difficult times. Sometimes it is a curse because I'd fall into that moment when I remembered how weak I was and how I had given up. I will not, not even for my enemies, pray that anyone is ever away from their children. I was nothing without them and from that day forward I would consider the four of us as one. We were going to become one unit and nothing in the world would be allowed to touch us when we were together. I had promised God that I would not ask anything of Him and I knew if I got my family back, it would have been endorsed by Him.

It was about one o' clock when I observed the minivan pulling in at the parking area for the park. I immediately got off the partially rusty bench in which I sat and paced my footsteps from one bench to another. I had waited so long for this moment because I hadn't seen them in such a long time. Whenever I look back at this moment, I would remember there was nothing else on my mind but Kevin, Linda, and Anna. It was probably the only time in my entire existence that my mind was blanked out towards everything else. If the world was on fire that day, I wouldn't have noticed.

A few minutes had passed and I heard the creaking of an opening gate. I turned my eyes toward the sound and I saw Anna holding Kevin's hand to her right and Linda in her left arm. In that exact moment, my eyes filled with water, my heart pounded, my knees went weak, and my surroundings became silent. They hadn't seen me yet as they were pre-occupied with various actions of activity in the surrounding areas of the park. They had all looked different, the same as I remembered, but different. Kevin had grown a little and so did Linda. I observed the tresses of her hair as it was blown into Anna's face. It had grown much longer than when I had last seen her. Kevin appeared taller and thinner and Anna looked meager and unhealthy. They all looked beautiful and it was a sight to behold. The camera in my mind had taken a snapshot of the three of them as they made their way closer to where I stood. Anna was the first to make eye contact with me. She immediately began to cry. I remember her lips curling up and the tears flowing and settling in the crimp that was created on her cheek. She put Linda on the ground because she clearly didn't have the strength to continue holding her.

Kevin then drew his attention to my direction and saw me. He looked at me, broke loose of his mother's hold, and ran towards me, "Daddy! Daddy! Daddy! Daddy!" he screamed as he changed into high gear and ran towards me. Linda then saw her brother running towards me and she began to cry but her hand was being held firmly by her mother. I knelt to the floor and Kevin crashed into me, and with my arms and his arms opened, I embraced him as he continued to cry. Strangely enough, I was happy that he cried. I was happy because I knew he remembered me, I knew he missed me and I knew I had not lost my son. Linda was let go of the grasp that held her from participating in the embrace of her father. Her little footsteps came running towards me and I reached out to her to join in on a father and son's embrace. She was crying as well and I was happy. I was happy because my little one, although it had been so long, had not forgotten who I was. Her tiny little voice called out to me as she mocked the cries of Kevin's calls, "Daddy! Daddy! Daddy!"

The moments in the park with the reunion of my family would become my most treasured memory. The snapshot that I took would be painted on my soul and till this day, I look at Kevin and Linda with the same passion and love that I felt that day. I had never felt closer or more attached to reality than I was during those moments. The bells of happiness had rung, they had rung for me, they had rung for Kevin and Linda and Anna. I knew this was meant to happen. The four of us together were stronger than any force that had existed. The bond that was strengthened that day would forge a relationship of familial endurance that would withstand the many hardships that lay ahead.

Anna slowly walked over to where we were with tears in her eyes and a humbled look that told me everything. Her eyes said that she was sorry, she knew that she allowed a wedge to be forced between us and she had vowed to not let that happen. She stooped to the ground and placed her head on my shoulder and her left arm around me. The four of us were united once again. That moment, there was a silence as a gust of wind that blew took the noises away. I could not hear the children in the park or their parents yelling after them. I could not hear the cars on the streets nor the horns honking. A calm surrender took over that particular moment and the angels gave us our deserved time. Time, it seemed, had halted, and we saw each other in our fullest glow. I knew then that my family was not a typical one. We were meant for something more and the invincibility of our bond was a force to be reckoned with. The moment Linda was born, there was a change in the world. She had completed my family, our family. Now as one, we were the conquerors and the writers of our own stories, the dictators of our own dreams, and no forces, whether of this world or another, were going to be stronger than the bond sealed on this day, within my little family of four.

I continued to give Linda and Kevin many kisses and embraces and continued to let them know how much I had loved them and missed them. They were small, thank God they were small, so they didn't totally understand what had taken place and there was still time to mend the time spent apart. We stayed on the ground for a few more minutes and then eventually would slowly rise and walk toward a bench where we all sat. Kevin and Linda both stayed with me. Kevin sat on my right knee and Linda on my left. Anna sat next to me. She did not speak much but she rested her head on my shoulder.

After sitting for a while, the emotional moments began fading away and Kevin jumped to the ground and started playing on a nearby swing. Linda followed and she came to a stop in the sandy area next to the swings. I was now able to engage and acknowledge Anna. I gave her a big hug and told her everything would now be okay. She continued to cry and said she was sorry. I told her to not worry and that what had happened was not her fault. We then started to talk and she told me how things were with Lucy and the others. She said she told Lucy that she was taking the kids to the park so she was able to get away from the house. Lucy kept a close eye on her and would monitor everything she did.

I asked her about the house and what had happened. She said that she couldn't remember everything, but she remembered one day they were moving and she didn't know why. Her mind told her not to but her actions were doing the total opposite. I knew Anna was telling the truth because I knew what I had been through. I knew that Lucy had done the same thing to her and she was being spiritually forced into accepting Lucy as her God, as her everything. Lucy had cast a wide net and both of us had been trapped.

I did not mention to Anna the information I had found out about Lucy. I wanted to tell her but didn't, I wanted to break the news to her slowly and at a different time and place. We spoke for quite some time while Kevin and Linda were making the most of a beautiful day at the park. There were other kids there and they quickly made friends while enjoying the activities and each other's company. Even though we knew to ourselves that we could not allow our meeting to come to Lucy's attention, we made sure to verbally let each other know.

After speaking for a while, we went over and joined the kids and participated in their childish adventures. We gave them turns on the rusty swing, ran around together, and relished every opportunity that the moment had provided. It had been about two hours and we knew that they needed to get going before Lucy had become suspicious. We called Kevin and Linda and explained to them that they should never mention that they had seen or spent time with me. Anna promised that she'd be with them all the time and that she would not give anyone else an opportunity to interrogate their whereabouts. I then walked them toward the car, placed Linda in her car seat, and buckled Kevin into his. Kevin had begun to cry before they pulled out but Anna and I both comforted him and assured him that everything would be fine and that he'd be seeing me very shortly in the future. He calmed down a little and they were on their way.

Chapter Sixteen

I returned to my mom's and happily narrated to them what took place and how the meeting went. They were all very happy but skeptical. They still did not totally believe that Anna was the old Anna and they somehow believed that I was still vulnerable to the evils of Lucy. I knew they wouldn't completely understand; they would have needed to be there in person to witness the personality and presence of Anna.

In the days that followed, Anna and I spoke every day, although not for long. We were planning on how to get her and the kids away from Lucy and her evil ways. We decided that we were going to get an apartment and find a mutual day where we were going to escape the clutches of Lucy. Anna couldn't really do anything due to her being with Lucy all the time so I called up various apartments for rent but couldn't get anything that was suitable for us at a reasonable price.

While going through the process of looking for an apartment, the bank that owned the mortgage for our house gave me a call. They said that the house was going through a foreclosure process and if we wanted, they could offer us an amount to relinquish total ownership of the home. I spoke to Anna about it and we agreed because we had no money to make the payments owed on the property. We set a day and met with the bank, and due to the equity the home had built up from the time of purchase, we were able to walk away with a few thousand dollars. We were happy to receive the cash as we used it to secure a short-term rental hotel in Long Island City, Queens. Anna and I planned for days about when and how she was going to run with the kids.

The day had come and Anna loaded her and the kid's personal belongings into three large garbage bags and placed them in the van. With her pounding heart, she returned inside, grabbed the kids, and proceeded toward the van. She buckled Linda into her car seat and buckled Kevin in as well. As she made her way to the driver's side of the car, Lucy rushed outside and asked her, "What are you doing? Where are you going?" Anna calmly replied, without hesitation or suspicion, "I'm going to the laundromat." It was an acceptable answer for Lucy as Anna had done so every Sunday for the last few months since they had left the house. Anna was scared, she did not want to arise suspicion from Lucy. She knew if she did, it would have most definitely spelled the end of all our hope. Lucy would have intervened with her wicked ways and resume her evil prayers to have total control again.

Richard and Daniel came running out of the house and joined Lucy at the car where Anna had stood. They began to question her as well. Anna was smart, she maintained her pretentious act of Lucy's control and told them that if they wanted to join her at the laundry, she'd be happy to take them with her. They looked in the back of the van and saw the three large bags and had no indication to disbelieve her. They did not catch on to Anna's timely bluff and told her to go and that they were not interested in going to the laundromat to waste their entire day. As Anna opened the driver's door, got seated, and started the van, Kevin shouted out the word, "Daddy!" Lucy and the others were about to walk away but immediately turned around when they heard his shout. Anna quickly placed the lever in drive, pressed the gas, and off they were. Daniel and Richard ran inside to grab their keys for their vehicle but hunted in vain as Anna, as clever as she was, had taken them along with her. She had planned, *we* had planned, for that event. I waited around the next block and observed the car peeling out from the front. As she drove further away from the house, I pulled out behind her and we were on our way.

After a couple of blocks, I drove the car in front of her and led her to the hotel in Long Island City in which I had secured. After parking at the hotel, I rushed over to the van and unbuckled Linda and Kevin. They were once again so happy to see me and we hugged each other before Anna and I took them up to the room. After getting into the room, Anna and I looked at the three trash bags, then looked at each other, and happily smiled. We knew the contents of those bags were all we had left, but we were happy. We were happier now more than we ever were. We were together once again and nothing else had mattered. *We* were all we needed.

We sat at the edge of the bed, along with Kevin and Linda, and we embraced each other and cried. We were together at this moment and we were going to make it last. We were going to make sure that no one would ever come between us ever again. A renewed strength of unity and togetherness had sealed our relationship with each other, and no forces, whether of this world or otherworldly, were going to be able to crack the bond forged from this day forward. The journey of becoming better than we were before had begun. We were starting over and we needed to distance ourselves from the negativity and from the evil ways of Lucy. I adamantly told Anna that she needed to cut all ties with her past. I told her if there was ever any indication she was involved or indulged with any of them in the future, that'll be it. I'd walk away. I'd take the kids and she wouldn't know where we'd be. I threatened her and she knew I meant every word of it. I had endured too much and wasn't going to go through the same agony again.

We showered the kids, put them to sleep, and I began to tell her about the information that was revealed when we were apart. Anna said she had heard stories, through the grapevine, that Lucy wasn't her mother, but she had chosen to ignore them. She had chosen to push them aside because Lucy was the only person she had known to be her mother. Anna had heard of Rachel, she had met Rachel, and she knew she had a resemblance to her but still chose to deny the evidence that supported claims of her being her birth mother.

Anna and I stayed up most of the night and talked. We looked at the sleeping kids and were ecstatic to see them happily together with us. We talked about everything and we were now on the same page, we were once again seeing eye to eye. Anna turned to me and said, "You know Lucy won't leave us alone." I told her I knew and that we needed to get protection, spiritual protection.

Morning came and we dressed the kids and went to breakfast at a local diner. While there, we contacted my mother and told her what had happened and that we needed to contact Mudeen. She volunteered to help us and she did. She called Mudeen and he was able to meet with us later that day. After breakfast, we took the kids over to my mom's where we were to meet with Mudeen.

After arriving at my mother's, she was so happy to see the kids. She gave them hugs and kisses and took them to the kitchen where she had the goodies they liked. She was happy for Anna and me but was still a little skeptical of Anna's past behavior. She did not fully trust her but she was making every attempt to be supportive and gave Anna the benefit of the doubt. They said very few words to each other because of her skepticism and Anna's embarrassment by what she had forcefully done.

The rest of the day, my mom spent most of her time with the kids while Anna and I spoke of our plans for the future. A while later, Mudeen showed up and took a chain that Anna wore and blessed it. He recited his prayer while twirling the chain within the palms of his hands. He then gave it back to her and told her to never take it off. She agreed and told him she was thankful for all he had done for me and all he had done to help her get released from Lucy's grasp. He told Anna that Lucy was the most formidable opponent he had ever encountered in the arts of evil. He made sure to tell her that I was close to being dead and she and the kids were close to never recovering from the webs of Lucy's unforgiving nature. Mudeen seemed genuinely happy for us and a relationship was forged through the help he had provided me and my family. We were also happy to have known him because we were clearly doing better, we were clearly emerging from the depths of hell, all due to the help of his.

Mudeen couldn't stay very long as he was to board a flight that night to return to Trinidad. Anna and I felt strong. We had been inspired by a man of great gifts and we had regained our aim, our objective, and our renewed zest for life.

My mom asked us to stay for dinner and we did. Whilst in the kitchen with her and while Anna was tending to the kids, she said that Nancy, Ray, and the others were also invited but had secretly told her they weren't going to attend. They told her they weren't quite ready to meet Anna and that they needed a little time. She understood and did not force them. She said they wanted to see the kids but they weren't going to at this time due to Anna. I told her I understood as well and that they should not be blamed for feeling the way they did. I knew with time everything would work out and they'd again become as close as they were prior to everything happening. We called Anna and the kids to the table, ate dinner together, and then left to the hotel.

In the days to follow, Anna and I resumed working while we hunted for an apartment. We had little money to work with and needed to be very prudent with everything we did. We found an apartment on 188th Street and moved in at the beginning of the month. We had stayed in the hotel for three weeks and lived out of the three bags we had brought with us. We found a daycare a block away from where we rented and started purchasing pieces of furniture and household items, little by little. We were recovering and we were doing well. Lucy had become a thing of the past and our little family had begun to flourish once again.

Chapter Seventeen

Three months had passed and we were beginning to thrive. We were beginning to save a little money and the kids were coming along well. Everything seemed to have returned to being the way they were, if not, better. We spoke of Lucy a lot but not when the kids were present. We knew Lucy would attack us if she found out where we were living.

A year had passed and we were living comfortably. I had utilized the money we had now saved and bought a franchised business in transportation. We also looked at a single-family home that newly became available on the market. Anna and I visited the house and fell in love with it. We were able to afford the down payment and we were in the house within six weeks of signing the contract of purchase. Kevin had become of age and was enrolled at the local school. Linda attended a daycare close by and Anna and I worked very hard to support the life we were now living. Everything seemed to have been working out for us. Everything fell into place just as we had hoped.

One Saturday afternoon, the kids were off from school, Anna

was off from work, and I took the day off so we could spend time at the park. We visited Sunken Meadow State Park in Long Island, New York. It was an absolutely gorgeous day – a little on the chilly side, but a gorgeous day nonetheless. Kevin, Anna, Linda, and I spent the entire day at the park where we had a wonderful time. The kids got ice cream, we ate food from what we had cooked and taken, and we enjoyed our walks along the beach. We collected shells, watched other people fishing, ran around the perimeter of the park, played badminton, walked, and talked. It was a very well spent day but it grew late and we had a long drive back so we left just before it got dark.

While pulling into our local street, at the corner of my eye, I could have sworn I had seen Lucy in a car passing us in the opposite direction. I didn't get a good look from the angle in which I sat but my brain believed it was her. My heart skipped a beat and a chill ran through my body. I did not say anything to Anna because I wasn't certain. Besides, if I was a hundred percent certain, I probably wouldn't have said anything either.

That night I became worried. I asked myself many questions, "If it was her, did she find us? Did she know where we lived? How did she find us? What are we going to do?" Many questions filled my head and I became somewhat preoccupied. Anna observed I wasn't quite right and asked if everything was okay. I told her everything was fine and that I was just tired from a long day and needed some rest. She didn't make anything of it and proceeded to bed. I stayed in the living room for a while and laid on the sofa just playing with my thoughts and memories, trying to convince myself that it was not Lucy I had seen.

As I lay on the sofa, I took the television off and was about to head upstairs to the master bedroom. The living room got really quiet as the sound of the motor from the refrigerator had stopped. The ticking of the wall clock could have been loudly heard and appeared to have an additional second or two added between the intervals. In the dark and quiet room, I looked into the corner of the ceiling and once again, the compassionate pair of eyes had returned. The eyes of warning had reappeared and had begun to weep. The walls were now lit up from the glowing tears that had trickled from the eyes that wept. I wasn't frightened due to the past experiences I had had with the compassionate pair. They stared at me with a warmth of despair and I knew they were there for me. I had become certain that it was Lucy I had seen in the car earlier. The eyes were my confirmation and acceptance that it was Lucy. The eyes were now gone and the walls remained aglow with the tears that had remained. It had become a beautiful sight to me, it was soothing to look at. A comforting feeling sank into me and removed my fear from the thoughts of Lucy. I wasn't afraid of her anymore and knew she couldn't hurt us anymore. The weeping walls reminded me of the time in the park when Anna, Linda, Kevin, and I were empowered by the love of our reunion. As the walls continued to weep, I admired its beauty and glow, I admired the stream of tears that had become my companion, my friend. The tears were telepathically communicating with me, to warn me of lurking danger and to assure me that I had the strength to go up against the evils of Lucy. I knew this day would come just as I knew the sun would rise in the morning. I was ready for anything to be thrown my way.

The compassionate pair had now returned and the tears began to recede into them. A slow and happy retraction was evidenced by the look given by the eyes. They had accomplished what they had come for and was now receding its glowing message. As the last drop of tears would enter into the fading right eye of the compassionate pair, it stared at me for a few seconds, and I knew they were saying goodbye. They had accomplished what they had set out to do and it was now up to me to maintain the strength and courage derived from their visits. They slowly disappeared into the darkness as I sat there for a few minutes, digesting the meaning of these weeping walls. I was stronger than I initially was. I had withstood the evils against me and the weeping walls had paid me a visit to secure my place as a conqueror. The strength, endurance, and love I had for my family had proven to be stronger than the evil Lucy had upon me. I had received an assurance from the weeping walls that my resilience was greater than I had believed.

A few minutes had passed and I checked on Kevin and Linda before joining Anna in the master bedroom. She had already fallen asleep and I did not want to wake her. We were all tired from a long and active day and I myself fell asleep rather quickly.

Sunday morning came and I was awakened by Kevin, who had jumped up on the bed and laid on my chest. The noises of the clanging pans coming from the kitchen could have been heard through the thin ceilings of the house. I picked up Kevin and made my way down the stairs and into the kitchen. Anna was busy cooking and Linda played with her toys on the kitchen floor next to the dinette table. I picked her up and gave her a hug and kiss, walked over to Anna, and did the same. Anna poured me a cup of freshly brewed coffee while I placed the kids in the living room to play. I returned to the kitchen and gave Anna a short synopsis of what had happened and told her about the weeping walls. Anna turned to me, held me tightly, and began to cry. She was afraid that Lucy had returned into our lives and she knew of her capabilities. She was afraid for me, for the kids, and for herself. I gave her assurance and reminded her of the protection Mudeen had given to us. I told her about the assurance I got from the compassionate pair of eyes and knew that Lucy could not touch us anymore. I reminded her about the strength we had as a family of four and told her that I needed her to be strong because, if she wasn't, that would be when we would become vulnerable again. She understood what I meant and grabbed her sticky apron from around her waist and wiped her tears. She was also empowered from the memories I gave her. We both went into the living room, sat with the kids, and watched them happily play with their toys. Anna and I looked at each other, smiled, and without a word spoken, we knew that we were stronger than we had ever been before, and we were prepared to face all future challenges that threatened our family.

The End

Epilogue

In the years to follow, Anna and I lived very happily with Linda and Kevin. I eventually sold my business and moved to Florida where Anna and I both worked and dedicated our entire lives to the upbringing of Kevin and Linda. Anna started working at a reputable company and continued her growth as a person, as a mother, and as a wife.

Linda started college and is progressing very well. She is strong-minded, very intelligent, and very ambitious. She returns on most weekends to visit us and her happiness is evident from the moment she walks through our front doors. I thank God every day that Linda was very small and that she does not remember anything that happened. There were no residual effects from all that happened, with the exception of us being a little more protective than common parents are.

As for Kevin, he has struggled some over the past few years and went through some tough times himself. After the situation in New York, we pampered Kevin much more than we did Linda, not because we loved her less, but because in the immediate years after everything had happened, Kevin had terrible dreams and memories of Lucy. He remembered some of the things that were done to him so we spent a lot of time nurturing him into being his best and getting rid of the fainted recollections that he still possessed. Ultimately, we may have spoilt him a little too much and there are consequences for that, but I would have my son alive any day, rather than not being with him at all. We knew what was done to him and we comforted him to take the perception of blame away from us.

After leaving New York, Anna and I heard stories of Lucy. We heard that she was homeless, we heard that she was dead, we heard many stories, none of which were confirmed. In the summer of 2016, we heard from a family member in New York that Lucy had passed away. She said that there was no one at her funeral except for Daniel and that she had lived on the streets out of garbage cans before she was found dead on a street corner. I thought to myself if I was the cause of her demise or if it was Mudeen who had returned the evils she had done back unto her. I will never know and I do not care to know as my wisdom had allowed for an unconditional understanding. Richard had died a few years back and was abandoned by everyone he knew. He needed dialysis on a weekly basis and we heard that he had suffered greatly before passing on. The specifics of what he went through were never revealed and there wasn't anyone within our circle that could have known.

As for me, I will always carry the memories of what happened and it would become my guiding light. I have become more vigilant and skeptical of people. I had seen and heard things that defy beliefs of reality. I had witnessed an evil that shook the foundation of all I had believed in. I may never fully understand the purpose of Lucy's acts or why she did what she did but I do know that she was after Kevin and Linda. I will never know if she was the devil that manifested himself into her or if she was the devil herself. What I do know is that she was evil. Lucy was the epitome of all that was cruel and spared no one who proved to be an impediment to her wretched deeds.

In the years that followed our relocation to Florida, Anna and I were very cautious and we understood the power of envy. We understood there were things in this world that may never be comprehensible nor explainable. Through our own experiences, we knew there were people out there who possessed abilities far beyond our beliefs and understanding. Anna never spoke much of what happened as she did not remember much. I will never fully know what happened when I was bedridden as my mom and the others would never tell me the details and specifics. I will forever be grateful for my family for sticking together and assisting me in all the ways they had done. They were forced into a conspiracy of evil that shook their own religious beliefs and yet, stuck through till the end to ensure me of my recovery. I've asked myself many times, was it my own immune system that forced me into isolation, protecting me from the pains of reality? I asked myself if I purposely secluded myself to avoid facing a reality so obscured by Lucy's acts, that I placed myself in a cocoon. There were so many questions I asked myself but I knew better. I knew because I had seen, I had heard, and I had felt. Lucy had left behind a trail of her destructive path and in many more ways than one, she had enabled us to now be aware.

The compassionate pair of eyes that glowed its tears down the walls never appeared to me again. We now live our lives as normally as we possibly can. I had gained strength, wisdom, and clarity from the walls that wept. There are many things, smaller things that happened, that were not mentioned nor that were told. I live my life based on lessons learned and from experience; and to Anna, Kevin, Linda, and I, we know there is no greater power than that of our little, but united, family of four.

About the Author

Bobby Karim is a simple person, father, husband, son, brother, and friend. He was born in Trinidad and Tobago and migrated to New York at the age of eighteen. He has since worked in the furniture and transportation industries, both in New York and Florida. As the previous owner and operator of a private transportation company in New York, he has gained great insight to understanding various cultures and ethnicities, that has allowed him to better communicate with his fellowmen. His most enjoyable moments are the ones spent with his family. His favorite words are, "There is no greater strength than that of believing in yourself and there are no obstacles that cannot be overcome without the unity of a family."

CPSIA information can be obtained
at www.ICGtesting.com
Printed in the USA
BVHW031056070519
547593BV00005B/85/P